BRAND-AID

Brand power at the heart of your business

Allan Bonsall

John Harrison

An imprint of
B. Jain Publishers (P) Ltd.
An ISO 9001 : 2000 Certified Company
USA — Europe — India

BRAND-AID — BRAND POWER AT THE HEART OF YOUR BUSINESS

First Edition: 2011
1st Impression: 2011

All rights reserved. No part of this book may be reproduced or utilized in any form or by any means, electronic or mechanical, including photocopying, recording or by any information storage and retrieval system, without permission of the author.

© with the Authors

Published by Kuldeep Jain for

An imprint of
B. JAIN PUBLISHERS (P) LTD.
An ISO 9001 : 2000 Certified Company
1921/10, Chuna Mandi, Paharganj, New Delhi 110 055 (INDIA)
Tel.: +91-11-4567 1000 • Fax: +91-11-4567 1010
Email: info@bjain.com • Website: www.bjain.com

Printed in India by
JJ Offset Printers

ISBN: 978-81-319-1083-2

About the authors

The authors have significantly different career paths and current occupations: one, an academic, has extensive experience in tertiary and vocational education, as well as experience with small business and social organisations; the other has a background in advertising, marketing and strategic planning, and managing and owning businesses. What we share is a strong belief in the value of a service culture and the important role of education and training in attaining such an outcome. Education and knowledge are never very far away from our number one priority as authors and in our respective careers.

Allan Bonsall spent the better part of three decades in the advertising business, climbing to the top of the corporate tree in Melbourne and Brisbane, before seeing the light and recognising that the advertising business and the PR business are just pawns in a much bigger game. Working with some of the biggest brand names in Australia, such as Toyota, Sheraton Hotels and Coles Myer, convinced Allan that survival for anyone in business could only occur if they truly pursued the philosophy of brands. *Brand-aid* is Allan's second foray into the business of writing and it won't be his last.

Dr John Harrison from the School of Journalism and Communication at The University of Queensland is an award-winning journalist and university teacher. He is the author of

Ethics for Australian Business (2001), Baptism of Fire (1987) and *Mass Communication & New Media: Broadcast to Narrowcast* (co-authored with Martin Hirst, published by Oxford University Press) and brings over two decades of experience in journalism and professional communication to this book.

Foreword

At the heart of this book is a very simple truth. Strong brands are the most powerful tools in our economy. We reckon that *most* managers still fail to respect that truth. They may well pay lip service to it, just as they pay lip service to the principle that the customer is king, or queen, but then conveniently ignore strong customer service for the sake of a little extra profit.

These very same managers fail to see how they can transform their business or themselves through the power of brands.

One of the most insightful business commentators of the past century was Peter Drucker. He admonished business leaders with the profound observation that without a customer, you don't have a business. A powerful brand is about creating such a strong relationship with your customer that they want to come back again, and again and again.

The power of brands is indisputable; there is real wealth in brands for their owners. The calculated *brand value* of Coca-Cola, for a long time the world's number one brand, is US$66 billion;[1] the brand value of Microsoft is US$59 billion. Brands are the real power behind the US economy, and in fact we believe that China's economy will never outstrip America's until China learns and understands how to deploy the power of brands.

Every business can build a successful brand if the owners and managers of that business are prepared to put their brand at the centre, at the very heart of their business strategy.

We are the first to acknowledge that the history of enterprise and entrepreneurship is littered with failed attempts to rebirth business strategy. After the Second World War, marketing was seen as the answer to the economic problems of the globe. The emergence of the baby boomer generation and the end of rationing saw commodities replaced by brands and the era of consumerism begin. Unfortunately, even in the 21st century, marketing has failed to capture the attention of the people who can either make it or break it: the strategy planners, who still pigeonhole the marketing department into a box on the organisational chart. The irony of this is seen in the small number of entrepreneurs and marketers who succeed beyond everyone's wildest imaginings, while the remainder, the majority, simply look at these great men and women, shake their heads and mutter something to the effect of: *That's okay for them; but it could never happen for us.*

Marketing has not been the only pretender to the throne. Jan Carlzon's *Moments of Truth* was a landmark in the service culture revolution of the 1980s. Many of Carlzon's ideas were picked up and expanded on through the late 80s and early 90s by purveyors of total quality management (TQM) as testament to the perceived importance of a service ethic. Like so many other business fads, even the concepts of TQM appear to have faded away, and now languish in the cupboards of Human Resources managers around the world.

There was talk of the service revolution, but it never eventuated because too many managers and business owners reduced everything to the objective characteristics of tangible products, with a view to maximising profit, essentially through turnover. Talk to a salesperson in a car dealership and the conversation generally revolves around the features you will get with a particular model. All too rarely do they try to match the benefits of the vehicle with your needs. Insurance agents will sell you a policy based on fear, rather than need. In truth, they have never learnt the value of looking at the customer's need, or more correctly, have not been *taught* the value of doing so, because it is a concept not understood by their managers.

If all of these managers were able to understand the power of the brand, and how simple it really is to apply those principles in their business planning, not only would there be a greater number of satisfied customers, there would also be many more profitable organisations around the world.

We believe that goods, services, people and ideas can all be successfully conceptualised, created and communicated as brands. The approach to business strategy we outline in this book will provide you with an easily understood and easily applied set of conceptual tools, which direct you to the starting point of any successful branding process — your customer.

At its very heart, *Brand-aid* is about how the concept of a *brand* assists you to understand the needs of your customers and turn those needs into repeat business.

If you are contemplating a future as an entrepreneur, or have already started on that course; if you are involved in the creation of high-tech products; if you are contemplating a career in which you can see a future that others can't; or if the bright lights of politics attract you — you cannot afford to ignore the power of a strong brand, and you can't afford to ignore the message of *Brand-aid*.

As we progress, we will explain to you what brands are, and, in particular, the emotional-connection imperative for a successful brand. We will also help you to carefully define the real purpose of your business and learn three powerful things: how you can add real power to the brand; how you can connect to your customers through your brand; and how you can think like your customer to understand the real potential of your brand. Finally, we will explore the ways that you can turn this understanding into a strong brand culture to make sure you always deliver on your brand promise.

The starting point for our journey is to understand that everything we do begins and ends with the customer.

Publisher's Note

Every major multi-national company understands brand building is an essential part of their success. Each one of them has learnt the secret to making it work.

The authors of Brand-Aid share a unique view of the world of brands. Allan Bonsall has consulted to MNC's in Australia and worldwide, working with them to build their brand. John Harrison has more than two decades of experience in journalism and communication, commenting on the phenomenal success of powerful brands. Together they share with you their insight into how brands create wealth, and how you can build your own powerful brand.

In Brand-Aid Allan and John unravel the complexities of successful brands and why a brand is more than just a logo, or a name. They explore the connection between the brand and the customer and how you can build that connection into loyalty and repeat purchase.

Today companies calculate the worth of their brand as a tangible asset. Building assets, or wealth, is what every entrepreneur, every businessman is looking for. How much wealth a company creates is determined by one thing – a strong brand, built on an even stronger understanding of the customer.

Brand-Aid is a book designed for your success. Whatever field or business you're in, here are the secrets to creating wealth through building a powerful brand that will have your name up in lights.

Kuldeep Jain
C.E.O., B. Jain Publishers (P) Ltd.

Contents

About the authors iii
Foreword v
Publisher's Note ix

Section 1: WHAT'S IN IT FOR ME? 1

1. In the beginning was the word.... 3
2. So, what is a brand? 11
3. Don't cry, emotion is the name of the game 17
4. The power of brands on the world stage 27
5. Understanding the brand's DNA 37
6. But beware, you don't own the brand 47
7. And what can become a brand? 55
8. Beyond queens and movie stars 69
9. The truth always hides behind the facts 77

Section 2: UNDERSTANDING YOUR BRAND 91

10. Defining your business 93
11. Drill bits versus holes 101
12. Six hats or one 107
13. What would your customers know? 113

14. We are talking about emotional ownership 125
15. Moments of truth... 131
16. Asking the right questions.. 141
17. Finding the right answers 153
18. At the heart of business planning.................................... 165
19. I have a dream 171
20. Adding value to the dream... 183
21. Committing to the dream... 189
References... 199
Index 203

Section 1
What's in it for me?

1
In the beginning was the word....

In the beginning there was the word. And the word was WIFM. The people began to apply the word to the things that were most important in their lives — Nike, Coke, McDonald's, iPods and Apple, Google, and Facebook.

And so it came to pass that the word became the mantra by which everyone existed and by which all decisions were made.

And the prophets — the marketing gurus and the communications seers — all said it was so, and developed their strategies to spread the word far and wide. And the meaning of the word was stunningly simple:

What's in it for me? WIFM!

Suddenly, in one simple question, you have summed up what Tom Peters, Ted Levitt, Peter Drucker and many other business philosophers have been trying to tell business managers for half a century.

Because the answer to the question "What's in it for me?" is also stunningly simple.

At its very core 'What's in it for me' is about recognising that you are the customer in everything you do, every waking minute of your life. Right now it may not appear so, but with that one blinding flash of insight you have the potential to unleash the serious power of brands.

And that's what this book is all about.

Every decision you make is on the premise of 'What's in it for me'. So, please, don't turn away from the idea in some sort of self-righteous pique, rejecting the selfish superficiality of such a statement. You cannot escape the fact that, in the end, every decision you take will have the ultimate impact — an impact on you. Sure, that context can be broadened to include your family, your workplace and your friends but it doesn't alter the fundamental premise.

So how does that knowledge benefit you? How can something so simple help you understand the power of brands?

There are currently more than 4 billion people walking around this earth who are making decisions every hour of every day that have an impact on their lives, their futures and the future of their families and friends. And they are doing it with the constant thought in the back of their minds: 'What impact will that decision have on me?' Or 'What's in it for me?'

Even charities understand the importance of the 'What's in it for me?' consumer sentiment.

Everyone loves the Salvation Army. It operates in over 115 countries around the world, including the most recently established army in Nepal, developed following extensive work by the Indian Eastern Territories. The sheer scale of the

Salvation Army operation is mind blowing. Its members speak 175 languages and operate more than 15,000 outposts, societies, centres and recovery churches. There are over 17,000 officers (clergy) and over 1 million senior soldiers (lay people). There are junior youth groups and senior youth groups and more than 23,000 corps-based community development programs. It operates social programs, addiction dependency programs, emergency disaster response operations, health programmes and education programs.

The Salvation Army has a reputation second to none. Many people don't know the full extent of its work and are only reminded of it at times of national tragedy when the uniforms of the Salvation Army appear in force to help the sick, the dying or the injured.

Each year, and in almost every country, the Salvation Army sits down to plot its one main fund-raising drive: the Red Shield Appeal. In Australia alone, this appeal needs to raise in excess of A$50 million to enable it to continue providing food, shelter and support to over a million people. Every year the Salvation Army provides over A$6 million in cash, food and accommodation to the needy. It accommodates over 10,000 homeless Australians and provides rehabilitation facilities for the same number with drug, alcohol and gambling addictions. Women in crisis and youths at risk are never ignored by the Salvation Army, and nor are those older Australians who are in need of a bed.

In Australia, the Salvation Army helps more people each year than any other single charity. The A$50 million dollars it needs to raise is hard earned in the competitive environment that charities operate in. Over 100 charities are listed as receiving community service support from the media, or in other words, free air-time or free space in the print media. Trends reveal that more and more charities are competing each year for funds from a dwindling pool of public and private donors. Around the world the competition is staggering. In Ireland there are over 5000 registered charities; in Australia there are nearly 9000 registered community service organisations; and Scotland has more than 20,000 registered charities. Imagine the competition the Salvation Army faces world wide.

The business of raising funds is tough. The business of persuading consumers to donate is made even tougher when you factor in public expectation.

That's right, expectation!

A few years ago the Salvation Army ran an advertising campaign in Australia for the Red Shield Appeal Doorknock that used the Australian iconic anthem, *Waltzing Matilda*. The fundamental premise to the song is 'Who'll come a Waltzing Matilda with me?' and refers to the Australian slang for travelling around the country on foot with your worldly belongings in a "matilda" or bag, slung over your back. Over the years the song has become the "unofficial" national anthem and is sung at numerous major sporting events, by an impudent crowd showing typical Aussie larrikinism and irreverence. It is a much loved song and most organisations and institutions would hesitate before using it as an advertising jingle.

The advertising agency working pro bono at the time for the Salvation Army (which, in Australia, is known as 'The Salvos'), decided to put sensitivities to one side and cleverly twisted the words of the song to ask: 'Who'll come if the Salvos don't?' The question was taken straight from the research conducted during planning for the annual doorknock, which made it clear that the public expected the Salvos to be there in times of need. In fact, it was almost taken for granted and was a blunt reminder of the need to resolve the consumer's question: 'What's in it for me?'

If the perceived single-minded and selfish premise of 'What's in it for me?' can have an impact on the Salvation Army, it's not hard to understand its power relative to more self-centred brands.

'What's in it for me?' has literally millions of interpretations if you think about it, and no matter what the variation, it is a fundamental principle that is hard to shake, and even harder to deny.

The Salvation Army understood the relevance of 'What's in it for me?' to its potential donors. Understanding that single statement, that little piece of practical common sense can potentially make the single largest contribution to the success of your brand, your business, your boss's business or even to you as an individual.

Still not convinced? Then let us explain it a different way.

What is the difference between *selling* and *marketing*?

Since Theodore Levitt asked this question in 1960 there have been many attempts to improve on his response. None manages to do it quite so succinctly.

According to Levitt, selling focuses on the needs of the seller and marketing focuses on the needs of the buyer.

The point of difference advocated by Levitt is significant. If you really want to succeed, you will only do so if you can get inside the head space of your potential customers and know what it is that they want.

One of the oldest principles in human endeavour is that current behaviour is caused by current beliefs. Therefore, if you want to change behaviour, you need to change beliefs.

Back in the 1980s, an international advertising agency by the name of D'Arcy, MacManus and Masius wrote a strategy paper called *Belief Dynamics*. At its core was the principle we've outlined above.

Current behaviour is caused by current beliefs. Therefore, new behaviour must be caused by new, or altered, beliefs.

All of a person's beliefs, rational beliefs as well as emotional beliefs, interconnect. And when the relevant interconnected beliefs interact, then the person reacts.

Or put another way: when a number of apparently unrelated thoughts come together, they cause certain behaviour.

But what, we hear you ask, has that got to do with the power of brands? What does it have to do with 'What's in it for me?'

Think of it this way. Each person has hundreds of thousands of beliefs running around inside his or her head. Groups of beliefs come together as clusters and can be identified as causing a particular behaviour. For example, the cluster of beliefs that may come together when you are considering purchasing a car will include the make, available options, price, status, colour and many other features. These are the practical beliefs, they're all important and they all make a contribution to your ultimate decision.

There will also be an emotional belief, which will make you wonder: How does this car make me feel about myself?

When the practical beliefs and the emotive beliefs come together in the right way, a decision to either buy or not to buy is the outcome.

That decision is at the very heart of every brand. Get it right and the power of your brand is multiplied tenfold, twentyfold.

To understand beliefs, you need to acknowledge the critical importance of the individual. When advertising copywriters sit down to write an advertisement they don't visualise a dozen people in the room. They imagine that they are talking to one person, a person who they can focus their attention on, and whose pattern of beliefs they have some hope of understanding. Equip the copywriter with the information needed to understand what is going on inside the target person's head, and bingo! You've got the potential to change that person's beliefs.

Simply put, if you can understand the power of 'What's in it for me?' for the individual, then with wisdom, you can transform what some may call self-indulgent selfishness into a tool with the capacity to build enormous wealth for any brand!

This principle was reinforced in a survey by *Business Review Weekly*, which found that "while business people admire companies for their management, finances and record of handling risk and adversity", consumers have a different emphasis. "Their direct or indirect experience of buying and using a product — and how well it delivers on the marketing promises — determines how they value brands," the report said.[2]

At this point we need to digress to explain a possible confusion that may occur as you continue reading.

Throughout this book we will refer to both customers and consumers. This is not because we couldn't agree on the right terminology, but because there is a significant difference between the two that is pertinent to the concept of branding. Heinz Baked Beans in the UK once produced an advertisement that purported to feature a very young Margaret Thatcher, now the Baroness Thatcher, and once nicknamed 'The Iron Lady'.

The scene is set some time in the early- to mid-1930s when Margaret's family owned two grocery stores, and lived in the house attached to one of them.

The commercial opens on a scene where a young girl, unknown to us at this point, is in the kitchen waiting for her breakfast. Her mother is at the stove carefully tending a pot. We can see an opened can of Heinz baked beans on the table.

After some dialogue about their hopes for the day ahead, and the mother commenting on the nutritional value of Heinz baked beans, the young girl pipes up, and says: *"If I eat all my baked beans, do you think one day I could grow up to be Prime Minister?"* To which the mother responds: *"You just might, Margaret, you just might"*.

It was a great ad, but more importantly, a very good example of what we mean by the difference between customer and consumer. In this example the customer is the mother. She's the one who actually selected and purchased the baked beans, for whatever reason or value she was looking for.

The consumer is Margaret; she's the one who literally consumes the product with the ambition of becoming Britain's first woman Prime Minister.

Often the customer is also the consumer. You buy a Gucci handbag most times for your own use. We will refer to the "consumer", rather than the "customer" because it has the broader connotation. Where we refer to "customer" we are specifying the "purchaser".

Interestingly, Margaret Thatcher's nickname, The Iron Lady, was conferred on her by the Russians during the Cold War. Many people don't know that she was also given the nickname 'Attila the Hen' by some of her British opponents as a somewhat more derogatory handle.

2
So, what is a brand?

Let's begin by agreeing what a brand is not.

A brand isn't a logo, a trademark or a symbol.

Neither is it any number of other descriptions of the many wonderfully graphic and clever depictions of company names. Unfortunately, there are still too many people who believe that to get someone to design you a striking logo and devise a clever name is enough to gild the value of your brand for years to come. What is even more concerning is that the purveyors of these beliefs are holding senior and responsible positions in marketing departments around the world, making decisions on behalf of their employers with little, if any, appreciation of the powerful asset they are holding in their hands.

In part, this belief has come about because of a number of confusing definitions of brand that have been paraded in the past. According to Keller (1996)[3], a brand was a name, term, sign, symbol or design intended to identify the product or service of one seller or group of sellers, and to differentiate them from those of competitors.

This part of the definition is misleading; partly right, but also partly wrong. But to appreciate the relevance of this observation we need to have a clear understanding of marketing.

The business of marketing is largely the business of brand building. This definition came from Phillip Kotler, American marketing guru, author, and a Kellogg Marketer of the Year. Kotler's books on marketing have been required texts for many business courses on marketing and market strategy for the past three decades.

Kotler says that when something is not a brand, it is most likely viewed as a commodity, and as soon as something is seen as a commodity, the only thing that counts is price. When there is no other criterion in the buying process, the lowest cost provider is going to win every time. Put a fancy logo on a commodity and it will make no difference to the outcome. In fact, the lowest priced product will still win. And there is the rub. Put a fancy-priced logo on a commodity and at some point you're going to have to add the expensive bill from the graphic designers to the price of your commodity. Immediately, and somewhat ironically, you have just made sure that your product cannot have the lowest price and you are on the way to building a brand, albeit with a long way to go.

Clearly, having a brand name or a logo to represent the brand is part of the brand solution. Keller got that part of the brand definition right. What Keller's definition lacks is the substance that sits behind that expensive, squiggly line, with the dramatic (and costly) silver foil printing. What the definition doesn't clearly explain is the relationship the consumer must have with the performance of the product, or what positive associations the product might have with something the consumer values, or whether it performs better than its competitor.

Many people have tried to answer the question: What constitutes a brand? One of them was Stephen King; not the author, Stephen King, but an Englishman who earned his money in the advertising business. King differentiates a 'brand' from a 'product':

A product is something that is made in a factory; a brand is something that is bought by a consumer. A product can be copied by a competitor; a brand is unique. A product can be quickly outdated; a successful brand is timeless.

If you think about it, that description pretty much sums up Stephen King the author. He is a brand in his own right. Consumers buy a huge number of his books because, while each of his books is unique, each one consistently matches the expectation of the reader. Imagine the outcry if Stephen King turned his hand to Mills & Boon. Almost every one of his titles has become a true classic, able to be enjoyed time and time again without becoming dated or irrelevant.

Another British advertising strategist by the name of Jeremy Bullmore defined a brand as a "complex set of satisfactions delivered".

Pointedly, Bullmore also defined a product as simply *"an object or service delivered"*.

Or a commodity delivered, as Kotler so wisely pointed out. Bullmore's description also rings true to Stephen King's definition of a brand as something *bought* by a consumer, not just something made in a factory.

At a conference on Strategic Higher and Vocational Education Marketing in Sydney, respected US higher education marketer, Bob Bontrager, defined a brand as being what the public understands and expects from 'you' (the brand) when they hear your name, view your images and encounter your marketing.

In other words, the brand is the sum total of what people think and expect from your product. This may sound on the surface to be a complex and confusing concept; however, get the brand right and it is one of the most powerful concepts in business, and is integral to getting your business strategy right.

Other authors have come close to this emerging definition of brand. Kapferer (1992)[4] saw that brands evolved over time and recognised each brand as a unique identity, one which evolves as the product develops.

In 1995 Upshaw[5] got it right when he said that a brand lived entirely in the mind of the consumer. He went on to argue that a brand identity is not what a marketer creates but *what a consumer perceives has been created*. For this reason, the brand message consumers receive will be dependent not only on the message sent by the marketer but also on environmental factors such as education, social grouping and other media messages.

Before we take the definition of a brand to its logical conclusion, we need to reflect on another critical business principle, and that is the definition of business purpose. In his book, *Management: Tasks, Responsibilities, Practices*, Peter Drucker astutely wrote that the only valid **definition of business purpose is to create a customer**. There have been many great commentators throughout the last 50 or 60 years who have influenced our thinking, and we will refer to many of them as we progress, but perhaps none put it quite so succinctly as Drucker.

Drucker was an internationally acclaimed business commentator, author and management consultant until his death at the age of 95, in 2005. Born in Germany in 1909, he moved to England before the troubles of the Second World War began, and finally settled in the US in 1942. He wrote 39 books, which have been translated into 30 languages, wrote a regular column for the *Wall Street Journal* and was a prolific contributor to the *Harvard Business Review* and *The Economist*. He was honoured with seven McKinsey Awards, the most awarded to one person. In 2002 Drucker received the Presidential Medal of Freedom. He held the position as Honorary Chairman of the *Peter Drucker Foundation for Non-profit Management* for 15 years; was inducted into the US Business Hall of Fame; and held 25 honorary doctorates from American and international universities. In his writings, Drucker predicted many of the major business and economic developments of the second half of the 20th century, including: privatisation and decentralisation; the rise of Japan as an economic world power; and the emergence of the information society.

His most significant contribution, from our perspective, was his extensive commentary on the decisive role that marketing would assume in all facets of business. By focusing everyone on the premise that the purpose of business is to create a customer, Drucker reminded executives around the world that *without a customer you don't have a business*. This message was stored away in the minds of thousands of ambitious managers because it hits the nail squarely on the head.

And the ultimate measure of a customer is the level of loyalty he or she shows in making repeat purchases, which brings us full circle back to King's — the English advertising Stephen King — definition of brand, the critical link to our beliefs system and how everything comes together under the power of 'What's in it for me?'

Consumers perceive the value of a "branded" product or service to be greater than the sum of its tangible assets. We can't always define the intangible aspects as accurately as we would wish because it is so individual and personal to each consumer; but this is where the promise of a brand, and the true power of a brand, begins to emerge. Brands build relationships. In fact, the brand is the very essence of the relationship built between the consumer and the product or service for sale. And relationships are the very cornerstone of success for any business because they represent repeat business.

Managing the image of a product or service so that it creates a desirable identity, which is greater than the sum of its parts, should be the ultimate goal of anyone wanting to create a brand. The aim must be to create a brand which, first and foremost, meets the consumer's expectation of 'What's in it for me?'; a brand that the consumer can relate to; and, lastly, but most importantly, a brand the consumer will want to keep buying.

We began this chapter by defining what a brand is not. We argued that a brand is not a logo, or a trademark or a symbol, or any of the other descriptors given to the depictions of company names. We challenge a number of definitions of a brand that have received a great deal of support over time but which failed, in our view, to capture the critical importance of the emotional and intangible relationships people develop with a brand. It is simplistic and dishonest to suggest that a brand is a logo because this assertion fails to appreciate the critical role of the individual consumer. Only when we understand the role of the consumer can we accept the obvious connection between the logo and the brand and the link it provides to the values implicit in the brand.

3

Don't cry, emotion is the name of the game

Consider the clothes you're wearing or the shoes on your feet. If you're wearing a pair of Nikes, ask yourself why. Is it because they are better made than the Reeboks your friend may be wearing? Chances are they were made in the same factory somewhere in Asia. Were they cheaper than the pair your friend purchased? Probably not; and most times it's difficult to directly compare one pair of shoes with another anyway. Nor was your purchase likely to be made because the colour of the shoe's trim matched the colour of your eyes.

Perhaps the real reason you purchased that particular pair of Nikes is because a number of people who you hold in high esteem are also wearing Nikes. Or perhaps the darling who lives at the end of the street casually mentioned how much she admires that footballer, you know, the one with the sponsorship deal with Nike. With enormous respect to your ego, we suspect we might be getting closer to it because the reasons people choose particular brands exposes the lure of the subjective, and how they view themselves.

Human beings are complex animals. That's how we came to believe that we are at the top of the evolutionary chain. Get hold of a good book on psychology and you will read chapter and verse about what makes us tick. In the 1950s, an American named Vance Packard wrote a book he called *The Hidden Persuaders*. It exposed to the world the apparently dishonest practices of the advertising and public relations industries which, he claimed, with a touch of theatre and moral outrage, were using the tricks of psychology to get inside the minds of consumers to better understand what makes them tick. By so doing, Packard's argument ran, the advertising and public relations people were finding different and devious ways to persuade people to buy goods and services that they didn't need, or didn't want.

The advertising and public relations practitioners reacted as expected. They were outraged to be accused of any wrongdoing, and far from being chastened, delved further and further into the human mind and the secrets of persuasion. Today, advertising agencies are exploring the use of neurological research to measure brain wave patterns and responses, all to gain a better insight into how people react to their advertising.

Of course, Packard was right. Advertising agencies were beginning to use psychology to better understand their targets. Do we find that morally objectionable, as Packard did? We think we should leave you to be the judge of that, but if they had not done so, the potential power of brands would have been largely misunderstood and we would probably not be in the position now of being able to explain one of the most fundamental reasons that brands work.

The most fundamental connection to brands is emotional, not rational.

In the days of Packard, more than 50 per cent of the population smoked. The habit was considered almost respectable, and if you don't believe us, watch the 2005 movie, *Good Night & Good Luck*, a story about American journalist Ed Murrow, his producer at CBS, Fred Friendly, and their role in bringing down the infamous Senator McCarthy's anti-communism crusade in the 1950s. Smoking was almost *de rigueur*, the required etiquette of the day, and almost without exception, every cast member complied. The set must have resembled a London fog, and talk of the potential danger of passive smoking must have been on everyone's lips, if their lips weren't already busy with a cigarette.

In the 1950s, 60s and 70s, people would 'wear' their cigarette packets as a status symbol. The brand of cigarettes you chose to smoke was actually a statement about *you!* Marlboro was western macho; Kool was simply, well, cool; Benson & Hedges and Dunhill held a mortgage on sophistication and understatement; while Peter Stuyvesant was your passport to smoking pleasure.

The fact that cigarette smoking has lost its respectability hasn't changed the need for people to seek out material extensions of their personality. For men, it may be the Tag Heuer watch on their wrist; for women, the Prada or Gucci handbag they're carrying, or even the Harrods bag they hide their walk-to-work sneakers in. You don't need to be a marketing guru to know why you pay five times more for a Gucci bag. It has little to do with superior workmanship or even better quality leather, although both features may be quite correct. Obviously you're paying for the name, and the gamble the top fashion houses take is to inflate the price beyond any notion of value, and hold their nerve. Their brand strategy is very simple: persuade enough people that they must have the product, make it only attainable to a few, and *voilà*, you have just put yourself in the same league as the major couturiers. The question is, of course, have you got the nerve?

Other brands take similar risks but for different results, and it is irrelevant whether the brand is a consumer durable, such as Coca-Cola or Nike, or a service provider, such as the Salvation Army, the telcos and the banks. Each one has a brand strategy that, first and foremost, is reliant on an understanding of the target customers' needs, but underpinning that understanding is an appreciation of the critical role of emotion.

No matter how many times your preferred supermarket changes its logo, chances are you will continue shopping there. And although you might try to persuade yourself that the reason is price, or location, or because they stock fresher produce, or perhaps a combination of all three, the truth is that you shop there because you have an emotional connection with that particular supermarket and it will take something close to an earthquake to make you change.

How do you feel about our outlandish claim that you use a particular chain of supermarket, or a particular bank, or a particular telco, or you choose Coke over Pepsi because of some vague emotional connection that has very little to do with truth or reality?

Consider the supermarket. Just about every one of them claims to have the lowest prices. Have you ever tested these claims to see if they stand up? Is the price differential between two supermarket chains really significant, or does one trolley of groceries cost about the same as the other? Have you prowled the aisles of two competing supermarkets with a clipboard in hand, comparing the prices on the shelves?

What about your bank? We would expect you to know the interest rate your bank charges on your home mortgage. You probably also know the rates its competitors charge. But what about the rest of your bank's products, do you know the interest rate on its premier investment account, or what it would charge for a personal loan?

In Australia, the UK and the USA, price comparison research between supermarkets consistently shows that the *total on the tape* at the end of the shopping trip for the same trolley of groceries is about the same, regardless of the supermarket chain. The Aldi supermarket chain from Germany claims to be different, and people who shop there will argue that the total on their receipt is consistently lower. However, anyone who has ever shopped at Aldi will recognise that we are not really comparing apples with apples (please excuse the dreadful pun) because the store does not compete with brand name merchandise, but offers, almost exclusively, house or generic brands.

Are we any closer to understanding the power of brands? Or how a brand could add real strength to your business?

We've read a great number of books on brands and branding, and often come away perplexed at the pragmatic approach and unemotional tone adopted. There will always be a chapter on 'emotional benefits' and as you read on you will find such a chapter here. But what we don't always find in the other books is a preparedness to actually try to analyse the absolutely fundamental role of emotion within brands.

If there is one idea you take away from this book, (although we hope that you will get more value than just one idea), let it be the maxim we espoused in the previous chapter: Brands exist for one reason, and one reason only — to create repeat business. Brands are created to make a sale, then to make a repeat sale, and another, and another, or at the very least, to gain a referral. Some brands are so greedy, they actually want both!

The thinking behind brands drives a philosophy that is based on **wanting** people **to come back,** not **having to** come back. Yet, the process of getting people to come back is not as straightforward or one-dimensional as it would appear.

Firstly, there are the physical, tangible reasons that may make a person want to return. The location is convenient, it's the only service in town, or the colour matches your eyes. On reflection, are these really that tangible, or is there a degree of emotion tied up somewhere? Perhaps if something has a monopoly then we could accept that as the driving motivator, but the rest?

Why do you donate to one charity over another? We've already looked at the case of the Salvation Army Red Shield Appeal and agreed that the Salvation Army is irrefutably a brand. Most people who donate to such a charity do so because they have a fundamental belief that the charity can actually do some good, that it can make a difference.

People also donate to charities because of a personal association. Cancer touches everyone in the world in some way. Sadly, we are all certain to know of a family member, or a friend or a business associate who has had cancer. If they die, we grieve for them and the next time we are asked to donate to a particular charity dealing with cancer, we open our wallets and purses without hesitation. If they survive the ordeal, we don't shy away from the request to give; in many cases we probably double the offering in thanks for their survival.

Whether you donated because you believed the particular charity could do some good or because it became very personal, these are not reasons grounded in fact. Can you put your hand on your heart and say that you can describe accurately what the charity actually does with your money?

In 2008 there were more than three billion mobile phone subscribers around the world,[6] with many of the mature markets already exceeding 100 per cent penetration. We're guessing that you own and use a mobile or cell phone, but what made you choose one telco or provider over another? Price, reliability, the package or the equipment offered? Or is it similar to the case of the supermarkets, in which the decision is a complicated mix of all the above.

Perhaps we should ask the question a different way. When was the last time you changed providers, and why? Was there something that made you angry about your provider? Did it fail to deliver on a promise, was it a lack of service (as is often the complaint), did the provider let you down or just leave you frustrated? When someone decides to leave an existing provider for another, 9 times out of 10 the reason will be an emotional one. Very rarely is the decision a practical one.

The emotional response to service, or the lack thereof, is a minefield for service organisations. Westpac Bank recently admitted that its decades-long strategy of closing branches and centralising loan approvals was wrong. It publicly acknowledged its mistake and in an attempt to redress those mistakes, Westpac has revived a key role long thought extinct — the true bank manager focused on local customers and their communities.

Westpac acknowledged through the media that closing branches had been a complete failure and that this was an admission the bank needed to make before hiring 400 new bank managers with the brief to be more hands-on, giving them more autonomy, and requiring them to be more active in their local communities.[7]

An online comment from an anonymous Westpac staff member had some empathy with the customers: *"...We are doing our best to 'delight our customers'. Yes it is 20 years too late and a lot of people have lost trust — (but) late is better than never."*

The bottom line here is that we are not dealing with just a physical connection, but an emotional connection between the brand and the consumer, and it is sometimes very difficult to get a handle on an intangible such as an emotion.

Which is why the business of marketing is largely the business of brand building; and a large part of marketing is communicating intangibles.

Think about some of the great advertising campaigns that you've seen. Each year, the pinnacle of advertising awards, the Gold Lions, are handed out at a ceremony in Cannes. The famous French resort town has become a mecca for advertising practitioners, just as it has for those in the movie world. Watch the most recent award winning commercials on YouTube. You will find commercials from different countries around the globe, and regardless of language, the great ads will always resonate. Why? Because great advertising is the visible part of the brand's emotional connection with the audience, and if it works, that connection is very hard to shake from the grey matter.

There are so many great examples of what we're talking about, where do you start? Everybody has an all-time favourite advertisement, even if they won't admit to something as crass as watching advertising, or even worse, being influenced by it. Television stations not only make money from advertising, they have also recognised its capacity to draw an audience and have created programs that air the world's best, or the world's naughtiest ads; there are even programs packaged as critiques, or insights into the world of advertising. The authors of this book appear regularly on a radio program, the title of which we 'borrowed' from Vance Packard's legendary tome. On 'The Hidden Persuaders' we tear apart the 'spin' of advertising and public relations for the benefit of the listeners.

As we said, everyone has a favourite ad. In 1991 a brilliant commercial for a brand of condoms named Mates appeared in the UK.

The scenario was simple: a young man walks into a chemist to be met by a smiling sales assistant, an attractive young woman, perhaps a couple of years older than our hero, and definitely not someone who our hero is going to ask for a ... a ... a packet of condoms. And, of course, that's what initially happens. But our hero has committed himself. So, here he is in the chemist shop to make a purchase, although to the viewer the focus of his attention is not immediately obvious. Confronted by the sales assistant he becomes suddenly tongue-tied. Instead of asking for the packet of condoms and getting it over with, he pretends that he is there for a completely different reason. He asks the young woman for co-co-cotton wool, and a pa-pa-packet of tissues, anything but the dreaded object of his desires, which might expose him as the shallow male he may be, interested in only one thing.

Item by item the attractive shop assistant complies with his requests until finally she asks: "Is there anything else?" What can he do? He's there, in the chemist shop; surely he's not going to hand over the money for his purchases and go elsewhere to relive the whole sorry business?

Finally he blurts out his real objective: "Do you have any *Mates* condoms?" he asks nervously, fatalistically. The shop assistant pauses and looks at him without emotion and then turns to the shelves, picks up a packet and examines it, unable to find a price. "Mr Williams," she calls to the pharmacist out back. "How much are these Mates condoms?"

In one sentence our hero is undone, brought down, left feeling ashamed and pilloried, all because he was a male, with natural male urges!

A brilliant advertisement; it was so right, and captured the reality of the emotions perfectly. It probably wouldn't work today, sadly, but then we're sure Mates have worked that out and are currently selling as much product as they can produce.

So, next time you buy something, consider your motives and ask yourself how much of the purchase involves emotional rather than pragmatic reasons. Do this, and you are a long way down the path of understanding the power of brands.

4

The power of brands on the world stage

If you still have any doubts about the power of brands, here is a very simple demonstration.

Find a low cost manufacturer in your category, probably in a developing nation and pay them approximately one-fifth of what it would cost to produce the goods in the West. Import the finished product into your preferred market for the standard freight costs; encourage the retailers to add a 100 per cent margin, but only after you have already set the wholesale price 400 per cent above your primary costs.

We don't have access to a company such as Nike's costing analysis, but in broad terms, that's what Nike does with every pair of shoes that it sells. Granted, Nike's marketing costs are substantial, but in that scenario, where is the wealth — with the manufacturer, the freight company, the retailer or the brand?

Therein lies the true business power of brands. The appeal of the brand seduces customers into purchasing, and then repeating the purchase, again and again, enabling companies, such as Nike, to maximise its wealth through its intangible brand asset.

By building the "brand assets", that is, the appeal of the brand or the desire to buy the brand, you increase the potential earning capacity of the product by three, four, or even ten times.

But the power of brands doesn't just rest with the companies that hold the brand. There is an argument that a nation's economic power can be measured by the number of "global" brands that country has. Further, that a country such as China could only ever surpass the United States as the world's largest and strongest economy when it can move beyond a focus on manufacturing capacity towards a significant proportion of wealth, driven by intangible assets such as intellectual property, proprietary technologies and products and, of course, brands.

There are two highly respected, but slightly different, measures of the world's top brands. The first is Millward Brown's *Brandz Top 100 Most Valuable Global Brands*. Over the past three decades, Millward Brown has grown to be one of the world's leading research companies represented in 50 countries and an expert and credible commentator on brands. The Millward Brown measure ranks the top 100 brands around the world using available economic and market data, as well as its own comprehensive study of consumers and business-to-business user's brand preferences.

If we look at a snapshot of the top 100 global brands, all but two of the top 10 in the Millward Brown measure — Vodafone (no. 9) and China Mobile (no. 7) — are US brands.[8] Vodafone is British, while China Mobile's origins are self-evident. Interestingly, the remaining nine brands are all iconic US brands, which perhaps reflects the current state of that nation, and the reason why the US dominates at a global level.[9]

BRAND	BRAND VALUE 2009 (US$M)	CATEGORY	COUNTRY
1. Google	100,039	TECHNOLOGY	USA
2. Microsoft	76,249	TECHNOLOGY	USA
3. Coca-Cola	67,625	SOFT DRINKS	USA
4. IBM	66,622	TECHNOLOGY	USA
5. McDonald's	66,575	FAST FOOD	USA
6. Apple	63,113	TECHNOLOGY	USA
7. China Mobile	61,283	TELCO	CHINA
8. General Electric	59,793	ELECTRONICS	USA
9. Vodafone	53,727	TELCO	UK
10. Marlboro	49,460	CIGARETTE	USA

We're not economists and don't intend to spend too much time arguing the principles or theories of that discipline, but the evidence in favour of brands making a significant contribution to a strong domestic economy is powerful.

In the US and Europe, companies with the most prominent branded consumer goods hold more than 75 per cent of their market value in intangible assets. For example, Microsoft has intangible brand assets of more than US$76 billion; Coca-Cola's are in excess of US$67 billion; and the McDonald's brand assets are worth an equally staggering US$66 billion. According to Millward Brown the most valuable global brand in 2009 was Google, with just in excess of US$100 billion worth of intangible brand assets.

On the other hand, among Asian companies recognised as brand leaders, the percentage of a company's market value represented by intangible assets is at best 50 per cent of the total, and more often than not, as low as one-third for even the most highly recognised Asian brands.

In the foreword to the book *Asian Brand Strategy* by Martin Roll[10], Professor Hellmut Schütte, the Dean of the Asia Campus of INSEAD, (originally *Institut Européen d'Administration des Affaires* - European Institute of Business Administration) argued that most Asian companies use price to push sales and, therefore, fall into the trap of becoming commodities. They forsake the value of repeat sales through the consistency and quality perception implicit in the brand promise. Professor Schütte went on to argue that few Asian brands are powerful on a global stage. Those that are come mainly from Japan, including automotive brands such as Toyota and Honda, and the photographic icon, Canon.

TOP 10 BRANDS – ASIA	BRAND VALUE 2009 (US$M)	CATEGORY	COUNTRY
1. China Mobile	61,283	TELCO	CHINA
2. Industrial and Commercial Bank of China (ICBC)	38,056	FINANCE	CHINA
3. Toyota	29,907	AUTOMOTIVE	JAPAN
4. China Construction Bank	22,811	FINANCE	CHINA
5. Bank of China	21,192	FINANCE	CHINA
6. Nintendo	18,233	TECHNOLOGY	JAPAN
7. NTT DoCoMo	15,776	TELCO	JAPAN
8. Honda	14,571	AUTOMOTIVE	JAPAN
9. Nissan	10,206	AUTOMOTIVE	JAPAN
10. Canon	8,779	TECHNOLOGY	JAPAN

Interestingly, none of the Asian Tiger economies, such as South Korea, Singapore and Taiwan, have products or brands that have made it into the top 10 Asian brands, and none is from the other emerging economic powerhouse, India.

By the Millward Brown Top 100 Brandz measure, China now has five of the top 10 Asian brands. According to the data, the China Merchant Bank's brand value grew by 168 per cent between 2008 and 2009. During the same period, ICBC grew its brand value by 36 per cent. The irony can't be ignored, nor can the implication, that few, if any, consumers outside of China would know too much about these companies.

At a briefing given by an Australian trade representative in Delhi during the 2009 global financial crisis, India's ability to weather the storm was attributed in large part to the vast population, which could consume everything that the country produced, and that India could produce almost everything the population would need. India's ability to be self-sufficient would hold it in good stead during the crisis but it also defines the premise of the potential economic power of brands.

Powerful companies in India do not need a market outside their own country to survive. AMUL (Anand Milk Union Limited) is a Gujarat-based dairy farmer cooperative with 2.2 million members, collecting 10 million litres of milk each day. The organisation's product line includes fresh and powdered milk, butter, cheese, ice-cream, chocolate and derivatives of these products, such as desserts and packaged milk drinks. Since 1967, AMUL products have been identified with a mascot, the "AMUL baby" — "a chubby butter girl usually dressed in a polka dot dress". The "mascot" or logo has been used with the tag line: *Utterly Butterly Delicious Amul*. In 2007–08 the company had a turnover of over US$1.5 billion. Yet AMUL's vision statement underscores the struggle by organisations in developing economies to become global brands.

AMUL is one of India's largest food manufacturers and one of the country's most successful businesses, but the concept of brand seems to be a far distance from its vision[11]. The vision focuses heavily on *commodity* language, and the producers or members of the cooperative. Although there is reference to its "respect" for the consumer, you get the sense that the company is more focused on the producer or product than on the needs of the customer.

We believe AMUL's product focus was never more evident than in its first attempt to enter the Japanese market. AMUL already had a toehold in a number of international markets in the Asian region and the US. However, its attempt to penetrate the Japanese market in 1994 was unsuccessful, due in large part, we believe, to the discerning and sophisticated brand consumers in that market. In other markets, for example, in the US, a large Indian population base would be natural targets for AMUL. Other regional markets would most likely be targeted on the basis of supply and demand, without an overt need for brand recognition.

An assessment of AMUL, written two decades ago by a group of US marketing observers suggested there were three reasons for AMUL's success: 1) a nucleus of highly motivated individuals in the early stages of institutional building; (2) a multi-disciplinary approach for delivering products and services, which is more effective than individual efforts; and (3) a leader with a very clear strategic vision.[12] No mention of brand, but a great deal of focus on leadership and the skills displayed by management in being able to scan the market for signals of decline as well as growth. In other words, looking for opportunities or threats to alternatively maximise or minimise market share. The US academics took this further when they wrote that AMUL *"not only increased its resource base but built sufficient flexibility to make growth possible at the next stage even while working with a radically different set of products and in different markets"*. The classic commodity market strategy confirmed that branding had little to do with the growth of AMUL.

Such a lack of "brand power" and reliance on commodity marketing is the problem facing emerging economies as they seek to emulate Western models of economic development. Yet, that aside, the top 10 Asian brands represent a formidable group. But are they significant enough, or strong enough, to challenge the economic power of the US and Europe as measured by the power of brands?

This measure of how a brand both rates and ranks is derived through a complicated formula based on the intrinsic value of the brand and from its ability to generate demand. The dollar value is defined by the compilers of the list as the sum of all the future earnings the brand is forecast to generate, discounted to a present day value. The information is collated from an extensive data base and validated through credible financial data.

It may be argued that emerging economies such as India and China, with nearly half of the world's population between them, have a large enough domestic market that they don't need to go global. On the surface the argument appears sound. With populations of 1.1 billion and 1.3 billion respectively in 2008, both countries could rely almost exclusively on their domestic market to survive.

During the economic downturn of 2008/09 India gave every indication that it could exist without international export markets, by relying solely on the needs and capacity of its own people to consume all the goods and produce it generated. That it managed to sustain economic growth at a higher level than any Western country during this downturn is testament to India's success in achieving this goal.

On the other hand, China is reliant on international expansion to consume its huge output, and while the strength of China's brand position now, compared to say, 10 years ago, is significant, this position is still heavily reliant on its own market and consumption from within. With the exception of China Mobile, China's emergence as a strong brand economy is driven primarily by the financial needs of a booming Chinese economy and the preparedness of China's leaders to assist other developing economies with funding to assist that growth.

To put this into perspective, consider another respected brand ranking. Interbrand's Best Global Brands also measures brand value using a complex formula of financial analysis, role of the brand and brand strength. Unlike Millward Brown's research pedigree, Interbrand's history and credentials have been gained over three decades as one of the world's leading brand consultancies.

There are naturally similarities between two lists dealing with the same subject matter, but there is one significant difference: Interbrand subjects its candidates to criteria that require the brand to have at least one-third of its revenues outside of its country of origin, to take into account the strength of the brand in the rest of the world. The Interbrand list contains nine Asian brands in its top 100. None of them is Chinese, seven of the top nine are Japanese and two are from one of Asia's emerging economies, South Korea. It is also interesting to note that only three product categories are featured on the Asian list: automotive, consumer electronics and computer hardware.

TOP 9 ASIAN BRANDS – INTERBRAND	BRAND VALUE 2008 (US$M)	CATEGORY	COUNTRY
1 Toyota	34,050	AUTOMOTIVE	JAPAN
2 Honda	19.079	AUTOMOTIVE	JAPAN
3 Samsung	17,689	ELECTRONICS	KOREA
4 Sony	13,583	ELECTRONICS	JAPAN
5 Canon	10,876	COMPUTERS	JAPAN
6 Nintendo	18,233	ELECTRONICS	JAPAN
7 Hyundai	4,846	AUTOMOTIVE	KOREA
8 Panasonic	4,281	ELECTRONICS	JAPAN
9 Lexus	3,588	AUTOMOTIVE	JAPAN

The clear lesson is that both the Chinese and Indian economies were built on inexpensive labour, which gave them a competitive edge in the commodities marketplace. Like many other developing economies, both countries have a rising middle class for whom commodities begin to take a back seat to the appeal of brands.

This fascinating transition is taking place in both countries. Wander through the shopping precincts of Shanghai and you will be assailed by every brand name under the sun in fashion, electronics, personal care and technology. In the Indian domestic market, where retailers were once "selling goods" there is now evidence everywhere of the importance of brands. That transition, from selling goods and services to promoting goods, services, ideas, people and places, as brands, is still in its infancy, but there can be no doubting that it is one of the critical markers of the transformation from a developing economy to a global economy.

5

Understanding the brand's DNA

"Repeat purchase" is central to the idea of branding. The concept of brand loyalty is central to brands, and the only way we can guarantee loyalty is to ensure the connection is never broken. But if a brand is both a physical and an emotional connection, how do we determine what those connections are? And which are the most important connections, the priorities that must be maintained?

Most of us will have experienced being let down by a product or service. Banks, telcos and politicians come readily to mind. We simply shrug off the experience and go back for more. Sometimes it is simply too hard to change our mobile phone provider even though we are at our wits end trying to work out how we came to be charged the amount on our bill each month. Other people are so locked in to a bank or financial institution that that institution can get away with daylight robbery and there is nothing you can, or will do about it.

DNA profiling is a technique used by forensic scientists to assist in the identification of individuals. The technique uses the DNA profile to establish a complex body of knowledge about the person, to know and understand the make-up of that person. Look at how the boffins represent the DNA graphically and you will see a series of circles, or perhaps squares, linked by interconnecting lines. The end result demonstrates the complexity of the DNA of each individual person.

A representation of a brand's DNA analysis would look the same. Each of the circles or squares represent the knowledge we need to have about the brand, and the links show how each of the parts interrelate to enable the whole thing to connect with consumers. The sum total of the brand's DNA would be the complex set of satisfactions that Jeremy Bullmore once determined the customer wants.

Brand strategists undertake a brand analysis in much the same way as the scientists examine a person's DNA. What they are trying to determine are the values that make the brand unique and set it apart from its competitors and turn the customer into a loyal purchaser. Brand gurus all have their own proprietary tools to help them and their clients work through this maze, to unearth the brand's real values and the experience that the customer is looking for.

We think of this analysis as determining the brand's DNA.

The first thing to understand about the brand's DNA is that customers don't buy the obvious features of the product or service, they buy the *benefits*. The oldest analogy in marketing is the drill bit versus the hole. People don't buy a drill bit, they purchase the hole the drill bit can create. Similarly, people don't buy electricity, they buy the heat that it provides, or the meal it can help to cook. Understanding this difference between *attributes* and *benefits* is the starting point for every successful brand.

The first perspective we need to take in our examination of a brand's DNA is to consider the brand's *attributes*.

Attributes can be rational or emotional, but they will always be distinctive, always competitive and, most importantly, relevant to the customer. Volvo is one brand that has consistently used the key attribute of safety as the defining point of difference for its brand. For Volvo, safety was always both a rational and an emotional attribute. However, the attribute of safety, as a point of difference, is only sustainable if it remains a significant point of difference as the marketplace evolves or changes, or the product category itself changes. Far from being sustainable, Volvo discovered that safety was only one of many attributes that people wanted from their cars. This became even more marked as the attribute of safety became an essential part of every other manufacturer's credo. The truth is, if your vehicle isn't safe in today's market you won't sell many.

Volvo's reliance on safety as a key attribute also had its funnier side, although perhaps not for the powers that be at Volvo.

Over a period of many years, Volvo drivers had become the butt of many Australian jokes, most revolving around the premise that only bad drivers bought Volvos because Volvos protected them from themselves. Pity the other drivers on the road. Hats also became synonymous with Volvo drivers, and the stigma attached to being a Volvo driver grew almost as rapidly as the number of Volvo drivers seen wearing a hat while they were driving. To counter this alarming trend the management at Volvo, which had monitored the release of Volvo jokes on a monthly basis, instructed that an ad campaign with the tagline *"Bloody Volvo drivers"* be launched in an attempt to shift a worrying trend that was having a significant impact on sales, by taking a light-hearted dig at themselves. Volvo also entered a vehicle in the highly rated Super Touring championship to compete head-to-head with the muscled up and macho V8 Fords and Holdens. And to cap off the campaign Volvo issued every member of its sales staff with a nametag, bearing the wearer's name and the offer: *"I'm here to bloody help you"*.

The managing director of Volvo Australia acknowledged in an interview with *Drive* magazine that Volvo attracted buyers who were frightened of having an accident and saw in Volvo's safety message their own salvation. These were drivers who often lacked confidence in their own abilities as drivers, but naturally wanted to survive an accident.

On the one hand, Volvo held the high ground on safety, but the same attribute was biting the company hard where it hurt most, on the sales chart. Research was telling Volvo management loud and clear that customers didn't like or welcome the ribbing they were getting at work or from friends when it was discovered they were a Volvo driver. *"Where's your hat?"* would be the most common question asked by these non-feeling, so-called friends.

The second perspective of a brand's DNA analysis is to identify *benefits*.

Essentially benefits are the interpretation of each attribute into a benefit for the consumer (the basis of WIFM). There are some products that roll out a plethora of brand benefits. McDonald's is currently ramming health benefits down its consumers' throats quicker than Big Macs, in order to rebuild an image that has taken a hammering in countries where obesity and poor eating habits are adding massive costs to the nation's health bill. Health is one of our core values; benefits built around core values are very powerful because here the emotional connection is that it "is", or "will be" good for me.

However, be careful. We need to be very clear about the difference between benefits and 'bonuses'. Mobile phones live and breathe bonuses. Almost every mobile phone promotion, whether it is splashed across pages of advertising, shouted at you from the television screen or confronting you on billboards as you drive to work, offers something extra — an added bonus that you can only get with this or that particular supplier. Sixty minutes of free calls or 100 hours of texting before you pay a cent are two offers that readily come to mind. In the strictest sense these are, of course, benefits in terms of dollars or value-adding, but without any long-standing benefit that locks you emotionally to the brand. They are not true benefits because they will not sustain your loyalty to the brand.

The third perspective of a brand's DNA is to look at the brand's *values*. Values, not value.

Values are used to reinforce how the brand makes you feel about yourself. If a brand presents itself as having good, old-fashioned morals, then chances are your conscience will be clear in purchasing that brand. When a brand is prepared to back itself with a lifetime guarantee, chances are you'll respond positively to that benefit because it reinforces the value of trust. Expand the definition of values and you come up with ideals.

Integrity and honesty are often spruiked as values that organisations see as central to their brands. Other values may include warmth and generosity of spirit, perhaps the ideal of providing support or consideration; in fact, the list of potential values is only limited by your imagination. But beware if the values come from your imagination; if the values you are trying to espouse are values that you respect but find difficult to deliver on, the potential is there to do your brand much more harm than good.

The fourth perspective of a brand's DNA is its *personality*.

For years, researchers have been asking focus group participants to describe the product they are researching as if it were a person, or a car, or some other descriptor that evokes the idea of a personality. A colleague, who runs a very successful research company, once used the car analogy to describe the personality of a hotel chain. The hotel group that had commissioned the research study was likened to an up-market model Ford — a very respectable brand that offered its owners a level of comfort not found in the more basic models and a certain prestige among its contemporaries, but still a long way from the Mercedes Benz they desired to be.

Although it was not the desired image, the personality of this particular Ford was positive for the hotel chain. It was prestigious without being over-the-top and reinforced the value-for-money image that the brand fostered, albeit at the top end. That the customer didn't perceive Ford in the same class as Mercedes or BMW was, in fact, a better outcome for this particular group. The luxury-end Ford was seen as less concerned than BMW or Mercedes with the trappings of image and more concerned with the comfort and practical needs of the customer. The Ford connotation was much better suited to the business market the chain was pursuing. In the same research, the BMW personality was attached to a racier, more image-conscious chain that actively pursued a younger, trendier market, characteristics which would have potentially limited the opportunities for the chain that commissioned the research in the first place.

The final perspective on brand is the most important, and the most complex to understand. This is the *essence* of the brand, a complicated fusion of the functional and the emotional components of the brand that, if identified correctly, will bring the brand to life. And like any good novel about forensics, this is the point at which the scientific analysis of the DNA stops and the intuitive analysis begins.

Coke is one brand that has its essence down to a fine art. *Coke is it* has lived in the minds of so many generations it's hard to remember where it all started. For years, Coca-Cola has poured millions of dollars into lifestyle advertising campaigns that have effectively captured the spirit of each one of the generations it has been courting. Surf, sand, adventure and life experiences have never been far away from the core of those campaigns. Coke marketing has unashamedly tapped into the desires and ambitions of the youth market, whether it was in the swinging 60s, the 70s, 80s, 90s or 2000s. For every one of those decades, and each of the generations of young people that has brought them to life, Coke has been IT!

Nike is another that has captured the essence of its brand brilliantly: the proposition *Just do it* sums up an emotional connection with the brand, an attitude of mind that is irresistible for the target audience. This is not a brand built on pragmatic attributes or rational benefits but on sheer exhilaration of life.

Kingfisher Air was launched in India in 2005. By 2008, the airline had been named the most admired airline brand in the Asia-Pacific region in the TNS rankings.

The owner and founder of India's Kingfisher Air, Vijay Mallya is the essence of his brand.

Like Virgin boss, Richard Branson, Mallya is a larger-than-life figure, who consorts with the beautiful people, all in the interests, of course, of building his brand. When he was asked about the reaction of his wife to his regularly being photographed in the company of glamorous women, Mallya told TV personality Lillette Dubey: "She understands my business and my personality. She lets me do what I need to do. I'm a brand ambassador for my brands. These are associated with 'high life'". Of his positioning of Kingfisher, Mallya says: "We have broken the shackles of conservative socialism. The growing middle classes want the kind of standard of living you enjoy in the West. So what I'm selling is a lifestyle". Mallya is definitely not in the business of selling airline tickets; he's selling an experience — that emotional difference between a product and a brand.

We now have a checklist of all the component parts of the brand's DNA that we need to address from a consumer perspective. Now we need to put it all together as a simple demonstration of what we're talking about. The example we intend to explore is the DNA of a tree, an example developed by the advertising industry in Australia to demonstrate this premise to students through the Communication Council's Ad School.

The attributes of a tree are numerous: it is a big leafy structure with a hard woody trunk; it has the capacity to turn carbon dioxide into oxygen; it is generally green; and it always bears nuts.

Convert those attributes into benefits and you realise that the tree can provide shelter, either as it stands or through building materials; it helps the planet breathe; it is serene; and it provides food.

The values of a tree are clear: a tree is kind, it is strong, it has a sense of spirituality and it is generous.

The personality of a tree is equally clear: it is motherly, undemanding, stoic and dependable.

Collectively, the essence of the tree could well be summed up as a *supporter of life,* an incredibly powerful emotional connection that has the capacity to turn the humble tree into a powerful brand, with positive attributes, strong benefits, high organisational values and an engaging personality.

6

But beware, you don't own the brand

Imagine the look on people's faces after they have invested blood, sweat and lots of money into creating a powerful brand, been congratulated on their endeavours and are then told that they don't own it.

"Who does, then?" is the usually irate reply.

The correct answer, ***the customer***, doesn't always pacify the brand's creator.

But, think about it. Who controls the purchase decision: the owner of the brand, or the person with the cash or credit card? It's really a no-brainer. The owner of the brand can do everything possible to make you purchase, but at the end of the day the decision is entirely yours as the customer. That's where Theodore Levitt's famous distinction between selling and marketing comes into its own. Levitt wrote that *"selling focuses on the needs of the seller, marketing on the needs of the buyer"*, and nowhere is this more evident than in the purchase decision about brands.

Many authors have argued that a brand lives entirely in the mind of the consumer and that a brand's identity is not what a marketer creates but what a consumer perceives has been created.

This is the very heart of the brand and regardless of King's definition, or Bullmore's, the most complete description of a brand that you will ever find, is the following:

A brand is the relationship between the consumer and the product or service being offered, and the strength of that relationship is measured by the loyalty shown in repeat purchase.

Who wrote that? Allan Bonsall and John Harrison, your authors, is who.

Think of all the other definitions, and what we've been saying, and we think you will agree that the ultimate aim of branding is to manage the image of a product or service in such a way that it creates an identity that consumers want to relate to and, in turn, continue to purchase.

Clearly the consumer is in control of that relationship, not the product or service, because it is entirely the consumer's right to reject the notion of repeat purchase.

A great brand only exists because of the strength of response by the consumer to its promise. The people who create great brands know that their wealth is in that same response, and that they can only protect that wealth while they continue to deliver what the consumer wants in a consistent manner. And sometimes that isn't as easy as it looks.

Last century, Americans and Australians were introduced to images of men, women and children, leaping into the air, their hands waving above their heads, all with joyous rapture etched onto their faces. The object of their unbridled joy was not a religious icon but a motor car.

And not just one car, but a range of cars.

We watched people jump for joy over big cars, small cars and medium-sized cars. They even jumped for joy about four-wheel drives and, later, they did it for vans and light trucks. Now they're doing if for SUVs and AUVs (as the latest literature informs us, Action Utility Vehicles).

So, what makes people jumping up and down like fools even remotely interesting for this book on brands? Why should we focus on a group of actors who probably got paid very good money to cavort at the end of a TV commercial? One perfectly legitimate reason would be the longevity of the Toyota theme: *Oh what a feeling!*

The first time we heard the line in Australia was in the early 1980s, in an advertisement for the new Toyota Corolla. "Oh, what a *glorious* feeling it would be to drive the Corolla," promised the advertisement.

Oh what a feeling, indeed, as the wife of one of our colleagues drove away from the dealer in her shiny new, fire-engine red Corolla. It was her first 'new' new car, at a time when a new car in most Australian families meant a car somewhere between five and 10 years old.

And it <u>was</u> a great feeling to be driving a new car.

As our colleague's wife parked it beside his aging, bright orange Torana, with the twin black stripes on the paintwork and the growling, powerful, fuel-guzzling V8 under the hood, suddenly *Oh what a feeling!* came to life.

Open the door of the Corolla and the smell of new leather would assail your nostrils. The smell of a new car surpasses everything, or almost everything. And everything that *Oh what a feeling!* promised was true. The only thing most purchasers weren't prepared to do was to emulate the actors in the television commercials. After all, they were paid to make fools of themselves.

As with most successful Japanese companies, Toyota set itself some fairly ambitious targets when it relaunched its products into Australia in the late 70s. One of those targets was to become this country's largest car manufacturer inside 20 years.

At the time, Ford and General Motors Holden (GMH) were locked in an intriguing battle to become the country's dominant manufacturer. A new addition to the GMH fleet, the Commodore, had been launched in recognition of the world's pressing fuel shortages in the 70s and early 80s. GMH set about building a marketing strategy that would ensure the slightly smaller, more fuel conscious Commodore would win over the hearts and minds of Australians. Unfortunately GMH executives got it wrong. Not all Australians were ready to heed the call for fuel economy and many loyal GMH owners jumped onto the Ford bandwagon, which continued to promote the Australian dream of owning a large, fuel-guzzling V8.

For others, perhaps the time was right. Certainly from a market point of view, things were starting to fall the right way for Toyota. And in that changing market what should be clearly understood about Toyota's strategy is that they did not set out to become manufacturer of the country's number one car. They set out to become the number one manufacturer.

The difference is subtle, but critical.

Toyota deliberately chose not to challenge Commodore or Falcon. Instead they positioned themselves to take the mantle as number one manufacturer, with products suited to the needs of a wide-ranging mix of Australians.

By the late 1980s, Toyota had achieved its goal, pushing Ford from the number one position and relegating GMH to third.

Unlike Ford and GMH, Toyota did not rely on one product to carry its brand. Its range included Corollas, Camrys, LandCruisers and, in the early days, Coronas and Crowns. Although each of the products was 'badged' and promoted individually, they were positioned collectively.

A critical plank in the Toyota strategy was the positioning of owning and driving a Toyota as a truly enjoyable experience. Exactly that feeling that is summed up by the expression on people's faces every time a brand new car is wheeled out from the dealer's delivery area. Much of that feeling is intangible, but it begins with the identification of a set of emotional values that sums up what people could expect if they purchased a Toyota.

Toyota's brand positioning, *Oh what a feeling!*, has been in place for nearly three decades and is inextricably linked with the promise of value associated with buying and owning a Toyota.

In 2004 Toyota became the first car company in the Australian market to sell more than 200,000 vehicles in a single year, 201,737 to be precise. This represented back-to-back victories in the annual sales race and was up 8.2 per cent on the previous industry record of 186,370 set by Toyota in 2003.

Toyota more than doubled its lead over its nearest rival, Holden, claiming the sales crown by 23,710, compared with a lead of 10,958 vehicles in 2003.

Toyota's vehicles dominated the off-road market, winning all three segments with RAV4, LandCruiser and Prado. Toyota's share of the SUV market also grew significantly, from 28.2 per cent in 2003 to 29.8 per cent in 2004. The company also continued to make ground in the passenger market, increasing its share from 17.4 per cent in 2003 to 18.3 per cent in 2005.

The message is loud and clear. No matter how big an organisation you are, establish very clearly what you want your business to achieve and what business you are in. Then, if you want the brand to perform, position it directly against your market's need. In the case of cars, much of the purchase decision is emotional. *Oh what a feeling!* captures the magic of that emotion perfectly.

Toyota has become the number one car manufacturer in Australia because it recognised the power of a great brand and captured the spirit of that brand in its slogan.

For more than 30 years the brand Toyota stayed true to that promise and has delivered a consistent product in every single one of the five brand perspectives.

- Every Toyota model has attributes that are distinct, competitive and relevant to its target markets.
- Every Toyota model can clearly enunciate those attributes into benefits.
- Every Toyota model reflects the values or ideals of the company, which are, in turn, reflected in the ideals of the prospective owners.

- Every Toyota model has a personality that is its own, and every one fulfils the essence of *Oh what a feeling!*
- If Toyota was just a logo, that strange design that contains three interlinking ellipses, how could it possibly persuade prospective purchasers to buy?

Clearly, it can't, only the sum total of the entire brand package can do that, and it can only do it with the permission of the consumer.

7
And what can become a brand?

In the previous chapter we defined 'brand' as *"the relationship between the consumer and the product or service being offered"*, and said that *"the strength of that relationship is measured by the loyalty shown in repeat purchase"*. We argued that the ultimate aim of branding is to manage the image of a product or service in such a way that it creates an identity that consumers want to relate to and are prepared to buy again.

So, on the strength of the above definition, what can become a brand?

We've already explored the power of brands on the world stage and put forward the contention that brands are one of the most important pointers to the strength of a country's economy. As unlikely as it may seem, Coke is not only one of the world's leading brands, it is also a symbol of the strength of the US economy (although there are many sceptics and critics of America who would say that Coke is part of the decline of US morality). Nike is another incredibly powerful US brand, as are Apple and Microsoft.

Many countries around the world have their own iconic brands that also rank with the major players. Finland gave us Nokia, Sweden delivered IKEA and Germany has given us BMW and Mercedes Benz as testament to its engineering brilliance. Japan has consistently delivered with brands such as Toyota, Honda, Sony and Panasonic. The UK has given us Guinness, Vodafone and the Queen, although only one of them ranks in the top 100 and the Queen may seem like a strange choice by some. South Korea has delivered Hyundai to the world; so far China has given us a bank; and the best known Indian brand outside India is *Bollywood*. While many countries might want to believe they have given the world a famous brand — for example, in Australia's case, many believe we created a global beer brand (Fosters), or an airline (Qantas) — in truth, these are brands that are very well known to the people in their country of origin but have some way to go before they can be truly considered global brands.

And in the scheme of things, does it really matter? Perhaps a brand's size and strength are important in some people's estimation. But to our way of thinking, the most powerful aspect of branding is the scope that it gives to all measure of things — regardless of shape and size — to build relationships.

Nor should we restrict our thinking about brands to the obvious product categories listed above. To do so bogs us down in definitions best left to marketing text books, although Kotler's definition of a product leaves our playing field fairly open.

In his highly respected text on marketing Kotler defines *product* as anything that can be offered to a market for attention, acquisition, use or consumption that might satisfy a want or need. Most products are physical entities that can best be defined as *consumer goods* and identified under a range of different descriptors, for example: *non-durable* goods, which are usually consumed in one or a few uses; and *durable* goods, such as furniture or a refrigerator, which should be expected to last. Alongside consumer goods are *convenience* goods, *shopping* goods, *unsought* goods, *specialty* goods and, not to be left off the list, *services*, such as a haircut or a repair.

So far we haven't mentioned the Queen of England or Bollywood, but we will come to that.

Many of the brands listed in these chapters are consumer goods, bought for personal consumption. They come in all shapes and sizes, colours and even tastes, and for the last century or so are most likely the only things that have come close to being recognised as what we now call a brand (social changes such as the invention of the Model T Ford weren't so much a brand as a revolution).

Coca-Cola began its long association with customers in May of 1886 when John S. Pemberton prepared the first batch of syrup, culminating in the product being the number one brand for most of the past three decades. The familiar logo was officially registered in the US Patent and Trademark Office in 1893 and ironically, much of the early advertising by the company was to try and dissuade people from asking for *Coke*. The abbreviation was finally 'officially' recognised by the company in 1941 when they gave in and began using 'Coke' in their advertising. The final capitulation came four years later when 'Coke' was registered as a trademark.

In 1873, Bavarian immigrant, Levi Strauss, and Nevada tailor, Jacob Davis, received a US patent to make men's denim work pants with copper rivets, and the name Levi's became an American institution long before the word 'brand' was understood relative to blue jeans.

Ivory was the name chosen by Harley Proctor, one of the founders of Proctor & Gamble (P&G) for the company's finest soap, following a sermon he'd heard quoting the passage "out of ivory palaces" from the 45th Psalm. The first advertisement P&G ran for Ivory soap appeared in a religious weekly in December of 1881, and it focused on the purity of the soap and the fact that it would float in your bath. The claim of 99 44/100 per cent pure was supported by a chemist, at a time when most soap was less than satisfactory, often an unattractive yellow or brown colour and likely to inflict more damage than it resolved. Ivory became a popular and well positioned product.

But did we think of *Ivory* as a brand in 1881?

Almost every country can boast a product or consumer durable that could be found on the shelves of grocery stores in the early 1900s. In Australia, a strange-smelling, evil, black concoction fitted the criteria of brand but was simply recognised as Vegemite, the stuff you put on your toast in the morning. Made from leftover brewers' yeast extract (a by-product of another iconic Australian consumer good) and various vegetable and spice additives, Vegemite is one of the richest sources known of Vitamin B and is most definitely an acquired taste! Just ask visitors to Australia their opinion of Vegemite and you will usually receive a very blunt response. However, even though it is not to everyone's taste, Vegemite has still managed to become a national icon, as much a part of Australia's heritage as kangaroos and Holden cars. A Vegemite sandwich is an obsession that has become a unique and loved symbol of the nation, the equivalent to an Australian kid as a peanut butter and jelly sandwich is to a kid in Pittsburgh;

rice or noodles to a hungry kid in Bangkok; a croissant with jam in Paris; or Danish pastries in Copenhagen. Unfortunately Vegemite is not quite as pleasant on the nose as most of those options and is an amazing case study of managing the image of a product so that consumers want to buy again.

Australian children are brought up on Vegemite from the time they're babies. For many years, addicted Australians would not leave these shores without at least one small jar of Vegemite in their luggage. Today, anxiety-fraught travellers can pick the product up in supermarkets from Bali to London.

As is often the case with any new product, the fortunes of Vegemite were not always as strong as they are today. In 1928, only six years after Fred Walker, a Victorian cheese maker, launched Vegemite, sales were slow — not surprising given the "unique" flavour of the product. In an attempt to put life into sales, it was decided to rename the product. Ever the frustrated copywriter, Walker registered the name Parwill in an attempt to help him take on his main competitor, Marmite. To understand the joke of the name you need to consider the advertising line that Walker developed to promote his pet product: *"If Marmite … then Parwill"*.

Unfortunately for Walker, the idea never caught on and the name was withdrawn in 1935 and Vegemite was brought back. Although his hopes of becoming a great copywriter were dashed, Walker showed his true flair as a 1930s marketing guru and introduced a clever ploy to generate sales for Vegemite.

Walker introduced a two-year coupon redemption scheme, giving away a jar of Vegemite with every purchase of other products in his cheese range. This might well have been the first product trial in the marketing history of Australia and the tactic worked; Australians tried the product and loved it.

The company continued to demonstrate an intuitive understanding of brand strategy by holding a poetry competition to lift the profile of Vegemite on the national stage. As prizes, the company offered a limited number of imported American Pontiac cars. Entries flooded in and sales multiplied. In 1939 the company gained endorsement from the British Medical Association to allow doctors to recommend Vegemite as a Vitamin B-rich, nutritionally balanced food for patients. But perhaps the company's greatest marketing coup was during the Second World War, when Vegemite was provided for all the servicemen and women on duty around the world. Supply to civilians was often limited to ensure the armed forces could continue to receive their rations. To foster consumer understanding, the company astutely ran advertisements depicting its commitment to supplying the fighting men in the jungles of New Guinea.

Today 22.7 million jars of Vegemite are manufactured in Australia every year, effectively putting a jar of vegemite in every refrigerator in Australia.

The Vegemite brand campaign demonstrates very well the way that a "managed communication" program can build the wealth of a consumer durable brand, but the question of what else can become a brand is still unresolved.

For the better part of 30 years, a brand has been developing under our very nose that doesn't fit easily into any of the definitions of products provided in this chapter. This is a powerful example of a new brand phenomenon and underpins our belief that just about anything can become stronger by applying brand principles.

If you're close to your computer, look at the brand names affixed to the outside box of the hardware. Right next to the brand of your computer are most likely the words *Inside Intel*. Now, every computer nerd will tell you that Intel make microprocessors and there has been a lineage of Intel micro processors since year dot. There was the 8086, the 286, the more famous 386 and 486, all of which enabled computers to become increasingly faster and responsive. Unfortunately Intel didn't obtain trademark protection on any of these numbers so the company was exposed to competitors who copied the technology and made their own chips.

Intel wasn't going to give up without a fight and in 1991 persuaded the major hardware suppliers to use the *Intel Inside* logo in their ads and on their computers. Persuasion came in the form of an advertising subsidy of three per cent of the hardware manufacturer's purchase of Intel products. This figure climbed to five per cent if companies used the *Intel Inside* logo on their packaging. Over the first 18 months of the campaign Intel gained over ten billion advertising exposures, ninety thousand pages of advertising and an increase in recognition that climbed from 46 per cent among users to 80 per cent. During the first year, Intel's worldwide sales rose 63 per cent.

Not bad for something you never see. But that's brand power.

And here's another example of brand power that doesn't fit the stereotype.

A few years ago Paramount Pictures released a movie that cost it one hundred million dollars to produce. The movie was *Mission Impossible III*.

The first of the *Mission Impossible* movies was released in 1996. The second was released in 2000 and a third in 2006. The series is based on a television series popular in the 60s and 70s that starred a number of actors familiar to the market at the time, but who are relatively unknown today. How many of you remember Martin Landau, Peter Graves, Leonard Nimoy, Greg Morris or Leslie-Anne Warren, some of the stars of the original series?

The star of the movies is, of course, Tom Cruise.

What is intriguing about *Mission Impossible*, the movie, is that there are at least three brands in the marketing equation, all of which contribute to the success of the product. The movie itself is a brand; there is, of course, Mr Cruise; and finally there is Paramount Pictures. The real question is: which brand will give the movie most credibility?

The origins of Paramount Pictures can be traced back to 1912, although the first picture to be released under the name Paramount was in 1914. Paramount Pictures Corporation, based in Hollywood, California, is the world's longest-running movie studio, edging out Universal by a few months. As a business, Paramount comprises a group of investors that make a return from television production, theme parks, international film and television distribution, and theatre operations in Canada and Western Europe.

The Paramount logo, although having undergone some cosmetic changes over the years, is still recognisable by movie goers with its ring of stars around the peak of the Matterhorn. The name and logo carry strong brand values of reliability, entertainment and quality, while the powerful visual reinforces Paramount at the peak of the entertainment business.

Since it began, Paramount has been synonymous with stars. In the 1920s it was Swanson, Valentino and Clara Bow.

By the 1930s the talkies brought in names such as Marlene Dietrich, Mae West, Gary Cooper, Claudette Colbert, the Marx Brothers and Bing Crosby. Paramount became known as a movie factory, turning out 60 and 70 pictures a year, with much of its success attributed to the astute business dealings of the legendary Adolph Zukor who built a chain of nearly 2,000 theatre screens to show his pictures. He introduced 'block-booking', which meant that exhibitors bought a year's worth of Paramount productions in order to get the specific stars they wanted.

In 1940 Paramount was forced to abide by a government-instituted consent decree outlawing block-booking and 'pre-selling' (the practice of collecting up-front money for films not yet in production). Paramount immediately cut back on production, reducing its annual output of 60 films by two-thirds. Yet Paramount continued to attract stars such as Bob Hope, Alan Ladd and Betty Hutton, and with war-time attendance at astronomical numbers, Paramount made more money than ever.

In 1948 the US Federal Trade Commission and the Justice Department, still unhappy with some of Zukor's business practices, took a case of unfair trading to the Supreme Court, and won. Paramount was split in two, with the 1,500-screen theatre chain set up as United Paramount Theatres. Paramount Pictures went into a decline, cutting studio-backed production, releasing its contract players and making production deals with independents.

By the early 1960s Paramount's future was doubtful. The high-risk movie business was wobbly, the theatre chain was long gone, investments in DuMont and in early pay-television had come to nothing. Even the flagship Paramount building in Times Square was sold to raise cash, and in 1966 Paramount was sold to Gulf and Western Industries who installed Robert Evans, a virtually unknown producer, as head of production. Despite some rough times, Evans held the job for eight years, restoring Paramount's reputation for commercial success with *The Odd Couple, Love Story, Rosemary's Baby* and *The Godfather*. The company also bought the neighbouring Desilu television studio in 1967 and used Desilu's established shows such as *Star Trek*, *Mission Impossible* and *Mannix* as a foot in the door at the networks.

In the 70s the string of hits continued with *Saturday Night Fever* and *Grease*. In the 80s and 90s it was *Flashdance, Raiders of the Lost Ark* and its sequels, *Beverly Hills Cop* and a string of films starring comedian Eddie Murphy and the *Star Trek* features. Many of Paramount's successes were remakes and television spin-offs.

The *Mission Impossible* 'brand' is also extremely powerful.

First released on television in 1966, *Mission Impossible* ran for seven years and chronicled the adventures of the Impossible Mission Force (IMF), a team of government spies and specialists who were assigned 'impossible missions' by the unseen *Secretary*. Although the cast varied over the years, the main characters included: *The Team Leader* (Dan Briggs the first season, then Jim Phelps played by Peter Graves in the other six); *The Techno-Wizard* (Barney Collier (Greg Morris as Barney Collier; *The Strongman* (Willy Armitage played by Peter Lupus); *The Master of Disguise* (played by Martin Landau); *The Amazing Paris* (played by Leonard Nimoy) and various *Femme Fatales* (Cinnamon Carter, Lisa Casey, Dana Lambert and finally Mimi Davis). The series is best remembered for its predictable set pieces: the opening mission assignment announced via a prerecorded tape, which always concluded with the words, *"Your mission, should you decide to accept it ..."*); the leader's selection of mission agents from a dossier; the intricate use of disguises; a typical 'mask pull-off' scene near the end of most episodes; and the relative lack of characterisation.

The movies borrowed heavily from the original series in almost everything except the actors. This included the music theme, the plot set-up, the use of disguises and, of course, the all-pervasive secrecy that was so well depicted in the original TV series by the "self-destructing" briefing tape. Critics of the movies (and we should probably clarify them as huge fans of the original series) have been scathing in their criticism of the producers' lack of "respect" for the original stars. Even Peter Phelps and Greg Morris are on public record expressing their surprise and regret that they were not included in the movies.

All the histrionics to one side, the brand *Mission Impossible* is still powerful. It has survived the original series, the television remake in 1988 and the three movies. But, is the brand big enough to carry the massive budgets that the movies take to produce, and provide a return for Paramount investors?

Which, of course, brings us to Mr Cruise.

Born in 1962, Tom Cruise is not typical of the traditional perception of Hollywood hunks. He is five foot seven inches tall, and certainly not handsome in the dark, swooning style of Valentino. Cruise is more of the model established by the late Paul Newman, or even the legendary Alan Ladd, whose co-stars were required to walk in specially dug trenches beside him to hide the fact that he was vertically challenged. Yet, ever since Cruise burst into our lives from the set of *Top Gun* he has become one of Hollywood's most successful and best paid stars.

At the age of 14, Tom Cruise Mapother IV was studying at an old Franciscan seminary to become a priest. He was a deeply religious young boy, the only son of five children born to his nomadic parents. He had already attended 15 different schools in the US and Canada until his mother and her new husband finally settled in Glen Ridge, New Jersey. While in high school, Tom developed an interest in acting and abandoned his plans of becoming a priest. At 18 he dropped out of school and headed for New York and a possible acting career. The next 15 years are the stuff of legends. He made his film debut with a small part in *Endless Love* in 1981, exhibiting an undeniable box office appeal to both male and female audiences.

Within five years Cruise was starring in some of the top-grossing films of the decade, including *Top Gun, The Colour of Money, Rain Man* and *Born on the Fourth of July*. By the 1990s he had become one of the highest paid actors in the world, earning an average US$15 million per picture. Cruise is reputedly a kind and thoughtful man who renounced his devout Catholic beliefs to embrace The Church of Scientology and is one of the best-liked members of the movie community.

For someone who had ambitions of becoming a priest, Tom Cruise has strayed far from his roots and become one of the world's best known actor brands. But while every one of his films has gone on to box office success, they have not always achieved critical acclaim. Does it matter? For the first *Mission Impossible* movie, Cruise is reported to have made US$70 million. For the second, the figure increased to US$75 million. In both cases he co-produced the movies. As a brand, Cruise is a very bankable commodity, as an actor, we'll leave you to be the judge.

As for our original question: which of the three brands would we be banking on to ensure the best return at the box office? Again, we'll leave that one to you to answer. The only comment we would make is that the brand identity of Paramount appears in the movie for approximately three seconds, and it doesn't appear anywhere on the poster promoting the three *Mission Impossible* movies.

And, finally, to the British monarch and Bollywood, an unlikely combination and one which might just challenge our contention that anything can be defined as a brand. Or will it?

The king is dead, long live the king is the sentiment expressed at the death of a British king. It recognises that although the face, the approach, and the style will change, the fundamental values, the very foundation on which the monarchy are based, remain the same, because those are the values that the British people expect from their monarch. Sound familiar?

Bollywood is unique. More a populist classification or tag, Bollywood is not a description for all Indian movies but rather the specific genre of Hindi language movies produced in Mumbai. It is a blend of two words: Hollywood as the perceived Western centre of movie production and Bombay, the name used for Mumbai during, and for a long period after, British rule.

Not all Indians revere Bollywood, and many see the term as demeaning to the strong culture of Indian movie making. Perhaps people in the West once saw Bollywood as a caricature, and held preconceived notions of what comprised a typical Bollywood movie, but more and more we believe that there is a growing respect for the genre and the broad following it enjoys, not just in India but throughout Asia and the rest of the world. The popularity of Bollywood movies in Western countries is not just an outcome of the Indian diaspora, but is a reflection of the warmth, humour and sheer exuberance of the genre that people take to.

Is Bollywood a brand? Unreservedly, YES! The values of the brand are consistent: the consumer expectation of the brand is locked into the features that must exist in each movie before it can even earn the classification. Watch the smiling faces, or the long expressions of the people leaving a theatre after they've seen the latest Bollywood blockbuster and you'll never doubt again how powerful a brand can be.

8

Beyond queens and movie stars

If the simplest test of a brand's values is repeat purchase, then there can be no tougher arena than politics. Disengagement and distrust are two common ingredients in politics, and they all too often sound the death knell for a brand. Yet politicians and political parties are increasingly taking on the persona of a brand to help them win re-election.

Barack Obama, Gordon Brown and Nicolas Sarkozy are all brands. The latter's brand includes the bewitching Carla Bruni. Manmohan Singh, courtesy of his recent election win, has established himself as a modern day brand in India, although the name Gandhi will forever live as perhaps that country's greatest political brand. Kevin Rudd has fast become a brand in Australia to his own audience in much the same way the prime ministers and presidents of countries as diverse as Canada and the Netherlands become brands. Ignominy does not preclude a politician becoming a brand, a fact that Robert Mugabe of Zimbabwe seems to take perverse pleasure from. Perhaps the exception to the rule is China, where the Communist Party, not the president remains the dominant brand.

Consider the most recent election held in most democratic states throughout the world. How prominently did either the sitting prime minister or president, or the leader of the opposition, appear in the political advertising to persuade you to cast your vote for them? In almost every instance, both leaders are promoted as brands, as the sum total of what those brands stand for. In fact it is much harder to promote an ideology than it is to promote the perceived strengths of an individual. On the other hand, it is also more dangerous to promote an individual as a brand because you run the risk of the individual letting the people down, and in the process, diminishing the value of the brand.

Barak Obama demonstrated the power of his brand when he won the Nobel Peace Prize, less than ten months after being inaugurated as the 44th president of the United States of America. There was a great deal of surprise and a certain amount of cynicism expressed about the decision, with some claiming that it must have been the man's oratorical power that had won the selection committee over, because what, argued some, had the man done in such a short time to earn the award?

Perhaps it was simply in the power of the brand, and the *promise* that the brand would ultimately deliver.

When John F. Kennedy won the 1960 US presidential election, he gathered around him the brightest, the best and the most beautiful to launch his inaugural term. The commentators dubbed his new administration "Camelot" after the popular Broadway musical that regaled audiences with the marvellous legend of King Arthur and his brave and wise knights and their beautiful women. Twelve years later, David Halberstam, in his bestselling book *The Best and the Brightest* (1972) launched a scathing attack on how the US policy establishment under Kennedy had fallen into the Vietnam War. Yet this and other attacks on the legend of Camelot failed to diminish how brightly Kennedy's star had shone and how well his very own knights of the round table had performed.

Much of the legend of the Kennedy White House as a modern Camelot arose from the television debates of the 1960 presidential election campaign. JFK's performance marked the beginning of television's decisive influence on politics. His youthful, tanned appearance and his low-key presence saw TV voters give the debates to Kennedy against the pale, sweating and heavily-jowled Richard Nixon, whose five o'clock shadow was plastered with make-up. In contrast, radio listeners — who could not see the two men — awarded the debate to Nixon.

Though Kennedy's untimely death in 1963 may have perpetuated the Camelot myth, there is no doubt that many factors deserve recognition for their contribution to the legend. There was his glamorous wife, Jackie, and his youthful extended family, including brothers Robert and Edward, and there was the astute use the president made of the mass media, and his friendship with key journalists such as Ben Bradlee of *Newsweek* and, later, *The Washington Post*. When all of this came together with the imagery used by Kennedy's speechwriters, it created an aura of youthfulness, elegance, purpose and vitality or, to use one of Kennedy's favourite words — tremendous *vigour*.

Vigour became one of the key attributes of Brand Camelot. Even though almost crippled by a back injury, Kennedy's physical vigour was demonstrated in pictures of family football games on the lawn at Hyannis Port, the Kennedy summer retreat in Maine, and in pictures of JFK sailing. Similarly, his moral vigour was demonstrated by his war record as a PT boat commander in the Pacific, while his intellectual vigour was shown in his authorship of *Why England Slept*, his Harvard thesis, and the Pulitzer Prize winning book, *Profiles in Courage*.

But was vigour the brand essence of Brand Camelot? In part, the answer is yes, because the brand essence is often intangible, an emotional benefit that some may define as sex appeal, or just good old-fashioned charisma.

Of course political brands were not unknown before Kennedy. Churchill, with his trademark cigar, bowler hat and 'V for victory' sign was perhaps the best known political brand of the early 20th century.

Branded as a feckless, irresponsible media tart while a minister in the Liberal governments before and during World War 1, Churchill had been ignored, even reviled, during the 1930s. The attributes of what we now know as Brand Churchill were really only defined in the dark days of 1940, by Churchill's radio addresses and the press photographs (and cartoons) of him as the British bulldog.

Tenacity, determination and courage were the hallmark attributes of Churchill's brand. Unfortunately one of the other attributes was arrogance, and when victory in the war had been assured, this particular trait of the brand began to dominate.

In the US, Kennedy's predecessor Dwight Eisenhower was another powerful brand. He was a likeable, grandfatherly, military man who led the D-Day invasion. His most memorable campaign slogan was: 'I like Ike' — a statement that summed up the brand and the man perfectly.

Obama is considered to be as great an orator as Kennedy and has the power to persuade and influence. People around the globe watched his campaign to win the presidency unfold. His battle first with Hilary Clinton and then John McCain will become the stuff of legends. Whether *brand* Obama will achieve the same legacy in the history books as Brand JFK remains to be seen, but like Kennedy, much of Obama's success still lies in the promise, rather than the execution, and that is a dangerous position to be in, as we will explore in the next section of this book.

A final reflection on Kennedy and Obama. It is no coincidence that the Kennedy presidency followed the widespread take-up of television into suburban America, a medium well suited to the reinforcement of brand values and brand attributes. Indeed, it is arguable that commercial television was specifically developed to promote brands, thanks to its ability to examine the many intricate components of a brand that would only otherwise be available in person.

Obama used television to gain widespread awareness and appreciation of his ability to captivate and enthral. But, like Kennedy, he was also a man of his age and the new media presented Obama with a golden opportunity to gain the trust of the new generation.

The 2008 race for the White House that comes to an end on Tuesday fundamentally upended the way presidential campaigns are fought in this country ... It has rewritten the rules on how to reach voters, raise money, organise supporters, manage the news media, track and mold public opinion, and wage — and withstand — political attacks, including many carried by blogs that did not exist four years ago.[15]

In order to engage with a diverse target audience across a broad range of political issues, Barak Obama and other candidates employed a varied approach in 2008. This included traditional grassroots campaigning and the use of traditional media channels, especially television advertisements. By October 2008, Obama had spent US$154.5 million on 292,463 to air spots, over McCain's US$94 million on 217,384 air spots. And this was prior to Obama's "multimillion-dollar" spending on 30-minute infomercials on both CBS and NBC six days before the election. Even though television has remained the dominant source of news, and thus an obvious choice for broadcasting a campaign message, these figures probably obscure the underlying role of social networking and Web 2.0 applications in political campaigns.

While the tools available to candidates have developed drastically since the 1940s, particularly with the introduction of the internet, some communication strategies have been slower to change. In 1993, the first White House internet site appeared. In 2000, campaigns used the web as simply another traditional, unidirectional communication tool to reach the population. Senator John McCain was among the first to use email as a means of communicating directly with supporters during the 2000 election cycle. Email provided candidates with a new opportunity to employ viral marketing tactics and connect on a personal level. That is, to tap into and use a network of existing supporters to "spread the word" through their own social networks.

The Bush administration subsequently began redesigning the White House website, and during the 2004 presidential election, both Senator John Kerry and incumbent George Bush used the interactive capabilities of the web to facilitate interpersonal connections and tap into networks of people. Howard Dean's campaign was the first to use a web log, or blog, as a public mobilisation tool, providing hyperlinks that sent users to external media content. Readers could contribute to the discussion on the official campaign blog site and were encouraged to distribute campaign site content.

Social networking websites, particularly YouTube and MySpace, played an increasing role in the 2006 elections, providing a channel through which candidates could further access, connect and rally voters. And, after membership eligibility rules were altered in 2006, candidates were able to establish profiles on social networking site Facebook to which supporters could publicly align. It is reported that Hillary Clinton had 12, 038 Facebook followers in 2006.

The true potential for social networking in the age of Web 2.0 was finally realised in the presidential campaign of 2008, when the significance of social networking theories was fully realised.

We have said from the outset that almost anything can, and almost anything does, qualify as a brand. Whether it is a jar of evil-smelling black stuff made from yeast extract, or a smoothly spoken and polished politician, if the service, product, person or issue needs to build a relationship with the consumer, then it can be branded, and the power of the brand can be used to create advantage.

9

The truth always hides behind the facts

We wanted to finish this section by relating a story that we believe encapsulates all the important lessons we have learnt about brands, and then some. It is a story about two airlines.

There is perhaps no single industry that demonstrates the potential power of brands more so than the airline industry. It is an industry with a turbulent history and a passionate desire to stay *off* the front page of newspapers. But at its very core, it is an industry that epitomises the consumer's demand for sustainable, quality service.

The airline that consistently out-rates all the others is, without question, Singapore International Airlines (SIA). In its 60-year history, SIA has been the winner of more prestigious industry travel awards than any other airline in the world. During the 1990s, SIA was named the Best Airline in the World for nine out of the ten years in the New York-based *Conde Nast Traveller* magazine's annual readers' choice award poll. At the time of SIA's 50th anniversary in 1997, *Business Traveller Asia* declared that SIA was the standard by which all other international airlines were judged, observing that the airline consistently leads the industry in profitability and "rides through rough and turbulent times much better than most of its rivals". There can be no doubting the veracity of BTA's comments. SIA has had an impressive and continuous profit streak throughout its journey and has survived many hurdles: the fuel cost rises of the 1970s when prices soared by 900 per cent; rival competitor attempts to steal SIA's reputation; the Gulf War and the post-war period, which rank as some of the toughest in aviation history; SARS and Swine Flu; and not to mention two of the deepest recessions since the Great Depression of the 1930s. Yes, indeed, a very fine pedigree, built on the back of a fundamental promise of service.

Yet not every airline rates service as the number one brand value. For years Qantas has been regarded as one of the world's safest airlines, if not the safest. The airline's record for safety has been unparalleled through periods when the front pages of newspapers were the unwanted resting place for stories about many other airlines across the world, including almost every one of the majors. Of course not all the crashes or disruptions to service were caused by mechanical failure or error. Since the 1970s the rise of global terrorist attacks has never been far away from the minds of senior airline executives and officials.

Through it all, Qantas managed to keep its safety record intact by not losing a single aircraft, either through failure or force. This fact even made it to the movies when the autistic character, Raymond Babbitt, played by Dustin Hoffman in *Rain Man*, chastises his brother for suggesting that every airline has suffered crashes:

Charlie (played superbly by Tom Cruise) announces to his brother: *"Ray, all airlines have crashed at one time or another, that doesn't mean that they are not safe"*.

Raymond replies emphatically, *"Qantas. Qantas never crashed".*

Charlie: *"Qantas?"*

Raymond: *"Never crashed".*

Charlie: *"Oh, that's gonna do me a lot of good because Qantas doesn't fly to Los Angeles out of Cincinnati, you have to get to Melbourne! Melbourne, Australia in order to get the plane that flies to Los Angeles ...".*

Of course, Dustin Hoffman's character was right. Suffering with autism, but blessed with the prodigious, if somewhat narrow, memory of the savant, Charlie could not be challenged on facts or accuracy. When *Rain Man* was made in 1996, Qantas had never recorded a single crash on duty. Nearly a decade and a half later that record is still intact. Yet ask average Australians their opinion of Qantas today and you are more likely to get a response about service, than one about safety.

We stopped 50 Australians in the streets and asked them what they expected from an airline. The responses were dominated by aspects of service and price. Almost without exception, "safety" was a key factor, but not the "dominant" brand value. We have already reflected on the shift by Volvo away from the single-minded promise of safety that ruled the Volvo marketing mindset for generations. In much the same way, travel consumers have responded to the bombardment of promises of better entertainment, better food, more room and better planes, not to the detriment of safety, but on the presumption that safety was expected; that as technology improved and our responses to threats became more overt, the spectre of disaster became less of a confrontation, enabling us to turn our minds once again to the more pleasurable expectations (or demands).

In terms of service rankings, the Singapore Girl heads the consistency stakes. The airline may not win every award that comes along, but SIA consistently rates. In the minds of our 50 survey respondents we could not find the same favour for Qantas. They were talking about their own national carrier, and our respondents could not place Qantas in the top three of preferred airlines for service. Safety still ranked, but in terms of what influenced their ultimate decision, well you'd better be safe, or you weren't even in the equation.

We can only speculate on the fall from grace by Qantas. We suspect that part of the demise has occurred through minor engineering problems the airline has been dealing with on the domestic front for several years. Its major competitor, Virgin Blue, has seized on this opportunity and has been running an advertising campaign that highlights the numerous cancellations and delays that have frustrated Qantas domestic passengers for some time. Many of these delays are featured prominently in the news. A recent Jetstar flight (a subsidiary of Qantas) flying from Sydney to Melbourne was unable to land due to fog. The plane was diverted, not back to Sydney its place of origin, or to an airfield close by not affected by fog, but to Brisbane, a distance almost double that of the return leg to Sydney. People on board the plane arrived at their destination more than eight hours after their original departure time. They made it to their final destination, and the airline made it onto the front page of the major dailies.

Again, we can only speculate, but from a branding perspective you want to analyse why a brand that has been so strong, could fall so far. When you start to look, a number of clues can be found, but we are quick to add that as every good suspense novelist knows, there is always more than one way to interpret a set of clues. Most of these clues, in our view, point to a serious cost-cutting campaign by the airline, and of course, cost cutting, it could be argued, is the precursor to lowering standards.

So let's look at the clues that got us thinking.

When talk at the annual general meetings and discussion in the financial pages focuses on the share price, someone looking at the circumstances from a brand perspective may well speculate that the most important customer, in the eyes of the Qantas board, has become the shareholder, not the person who actually sits in the aisle seat in row 42.

Planes breaking down and being constantly delayed point to the likelihood of belt tightening rather than concerns about air safety.

Further clues can be found in discussions about relocating the servicing of aircraft offshore, or in hiring flight attendants in countries other than Australia. Arguments of political correctness don't wash (even though they may be, just that, politically correct) when you are reviewing the very things that have made the brand what it is: its character, its values and in this case, above everything, its very personality.

The final clue came in recent speculation about a potential takeover, which morphed into talks of a merger between Qantas and another major airline, possibly British Airways or Air France. Some sense could then be made of the Board's and the CEO's predisposition to, and fascination with, the share price.

Put it all together and we conclude that this is an airline focused on the bottom line, determined to trim away every possible piece of fat so that the share price has the opportunity to consolidate, even grow, and at the expense of what?

No, the simple answer is not service, that's the by-product of the cost cutting. Quite clearly, service must suffer if the instruction is there for managers to seek out every possible piece of excess and remove it. But the real answer to what suffers is the BRAND.

Everything about the brand is built on the values that you, as the manager of your brand, and your management team, determine is important about your offering, what will make you different and stand out. That doesn't mean you exclude the customers, quite the reverse: a strong brand is built on an understanding of what your customers want. But the decisions on how you offer that to your customers is in the control of the people building the brand. To our way of thinking, Qantas lost sight of that fact when it determined that it would be much better off as part of a larger international brand and set themselves on a course for takeover or buy-out. (Ironically the Board and the management team probably had very sound business reasons for doing so.)

You don't have to be the smartest business analyst to know that the world has changed and that operating circumstances for airlines are constantly changing. Hedging fuel prices on its own would be sufficient to turn any manager's hair white. Having said that, we wonder if Qantas would have made the same decisions if management had been as passionate about the brand as they were about the share price?

And the sad fact of the matter is that the brand didn't have to suffer.

At this point, our story goes full circle, back to Singapore International Airlines. The story of Singapore Airlines and the Singapore Girl is a fascinating study into a powerful brand that has weathered all the storms confronting Qantas, and managed to survive every one of them.

SIA is Singapore's best-known company, and is rated consistently as Asia's "most admired company". Its smiling, willowy cabin attendant, outfitted in a tight batik sarong designed by renowned fashion house Pierre Balmain, and marketed as the Singapore Girl, is now a well-known international service icon. In 1994, the year she celebrated her 21st birthday, the Singapore Girl became the first commercial figure to be displayed at the famed Madame Tussaud's Museum in London.

SIA is widely reckoned by those in the airline industry as one of the very best airlines in the world. It has had an impressive and continuous profit streak since it took to the skies some 37 years ago; a track record almost unheard of in the brutal airline industry.

For the purposes of the original case study, SIA was compared with and benchmarked against British Airways (BA), Europe's largest airline and widely regarded as a top international airline. By virtue of its unique history, Malaysian Airlines System (MAS) was also included as a comparison airline, not only because it is a respectable company by airline industry standards, with a history as long as SIA's, but because MAS also shares a common origin and history with SIA until their mutual parting of ways on 1 October 1972.

In 1947, Malayan Airways was established and operated services between Kuala Lumpur, Singapore, Ipoh and Penang. In 1963, it was renamed Malaysian Airways Limited and in

1966, the Malaysian and Singapore governments acquired joint majority control. The following year, it was renamed Malaysia–Singapore Airlines (MSA) Limited until the Malaysian and Singapore governments agreed to set up separate national airlines in 1972. From October in that year, Malaysia–Singapore Airlines ceased operations and was reborn as Singapore International Airlines (SIA) and Malaysian Airlines System (MAS), with MAS taking over all the domestic routes and SIA taking over the international network.

SIA immediately embarked on an aggressive program of growth, and aircraft and equipment acquisition. It acquired Boeing 747 Jumbo Jets, which went into service in 1973, and by 1979 had become the ninth largest airline in the world. SIA shares were listed on the Singapore Stock Exchange on 18 December 1985, and a new corporate identity was unveiled on 28 April 1987. On 14 December 1989, SIA concluded a major world-wide alliance with SwissAir and Delta Airlines, covering wide-ranging co-operation and eventual exchange of equity. An Memorandum Of Understanding with Cathay Pacific Airways and Malaysia Airlines was signed on 22 December 1992. By the time the airline turned 50 on 1 May 1997, it had already grown into a diversified group and a leading player among international airlines.

A key part of this growth was the decision taken within a year of the split from MSA to look for a new way to differentiate itself. In 1973, SIA had in its service some of the world's most modern aircraft. Its maintenance operations were generally recognised to be on a par with those of the world's major airlines. All its pilots and engineers were proficient and experienced, as there were no restraints from the unions on hiring Western crew members if SIA thought they were better.

The product/service differentiation strategy SIA chose was based on in-flight service. At the time, SIA's advertising manager summed up the strategy by saying:

What we needed was a "unique selling proposition". Happily, we found it. Or perhaps I should say we found her, because the Singapore Girl has become synonymous with Singapore Airlines.

SIA is an Asian airline, and Asia has a long tradition of gentle, courteous service. The Asian woman does not feel she is demeaning herself by fulfilling the role of the gracious, charming and helpful hostess. What we hope to do is translate that tradition of service into an in-flight reality.[20]

In a single move, SIA was strategically positioned in the premium service, quality and value market segment of the international airline industry. Passengers were treated to some of the best food on any airline, which is served with "lots of warm smiles, warm towels, and attention to detail". It provided first-class, business-class and economy-class passengers with cocktails, fine wines, and in-flight motion pictures at no extra charge. Service became the *raison d'être* for SIA, and at the heart of its service reputation was the Singapore Girl. Slogans such as "A standard of service that even other airlines talk about" and "SIA: you are a great way to fly" were used regularly in its marketing.

SIA has always been of the view that the key to its success was its "value or quality for the money". SIA's corporate philosophy was best summed up in the statement by Harvard Business School Chairman, Joseph Pillay, who wrote in 1989:

The airline industry is, by its very nature, a service industry. In a free market, the success or failure of an individual airline is largely dictated by the quality of the service it provides.[21]

Every airline has one eye on achieving the same ideals. Unfortunately none has been quite able to juggle the apparent contradiction between cutting costs and prices while maintaining a customer focus. Because of its strong market position, SIA was not saddled with this dilemma. While keeping an eye on costs, its "quality and service-enhancement strategy" allowed it to command a relative market price premium position through "premium service, value and quality" epitomised by the Singapore Girl, the idealised version of the SIA cabin attendant. She was the centrepiece in SIA's marketing strategy: always stylish, always in control, but always attentive.

In 1979, *Fortune* magazine featured an article "Flying high with the Singapore Girls". The story noted that "far from being repelled by the notion of becoming a 'Singapore girl', about 7,000 young Singaporean women applied for 347 openings in the hostess ranks of SIA".

Some 40 years later, the Singapore Girl appears to have become even more popular and entrenched. On a recent flight from Singapore to Brisbane I had the opportunity to speak with the male purser at some length. I asked him what the "Singapore Girl" meant to him. As I enjoyed the ice-cream he had just "discovered" in the galley, he smiled. *"Everything,"* he said in reply.

He didn't have to say anything more on that subject for me to understand, but he elaborated:

I am proud to be part of an airline that people acclaim as having the best service in the world and I am proud that we have never once deviated from the promise we make to our customers.

At the very heart of the purser's proud response was something integral to every great brand: a vision that aspired not just to being a good airline, but a great airline.

A critical part of SIA's strategy to differentiate itself on the basis of superior customer service, was management's ability to establish a vision of service excellence throughout the organisation. Ironically it was an executive from another airline, Jan Carlzon from Scandinavian Airways, who captured the importance of a company's vision as a part of the service ethos in his book *Moments of Truth* (more about Jan Carlzon later). Such an organisation-wide energising vision of service excellence is a powerful source of competitive advantage in top-class service organisations. A service organisation that does not have such a shared vision and culture of service excellence will have a tough task acquiring it, as it cannot be bought.

SIA's strategy focuses on enhancing quality or service and preventing customer problems from arising, not on reducing costs. That the airline has succeeded with such a strategy reinforces the lessons that many service businesses have learnt over the years. At the very core of a good business is the consequence of "repeat business" and referrals. Smart managers know that it is much more cost effective to build repeat business and build new business on the basis of referrals from existing customers, which is the bedrock of successful marketing.

SIA's bold strategic vision and the aspiration of being a top airline, not just a good airline, aligned with its careful market positioning and delivery of its service promise, virtually guaranteed that SIA would become the very first airline in the international airline industry to succeed with such a powerful and enduring image of quality service to build a sustainable competitive advantage. Its ability to sustain this advantage, even as its competitors seek to develop comparable service capability, had been buttressed by the fact that it was the first to earn and attain the quality-service position and image in the market and in customers' minds.

To support this strategy of service excellence, SIA adopted a rigorous quality control system and process for staff recruitment and selection, as well as a rigorous training and service policy. And all the while, SIA has had a virtually uninterrupted profit track record.

Only in the last year or so, as the world faced uncertainty through the global recession, has the profit light dimmed. Throughout the 1990s SIA maintained an upward growth trend, consistently setting profit levels that other airlines could only dream about. Even in the face of the doom and gloom being spruiked, the company is looking ahead positively. SIA maintains a comfortable margin between its actual and break-even load factor, and although the company's shares fell during the second half of the 2008 fiscal by 12 per cent, this should be compared to the Singapore index fall of 16 per cent, and comparative falls by Cathay Pacific and Qantas of 24 per cent and 36 per cent, respectively.

SIA strategies are not complicated or earth shattering. The airline has an established practice of keeping its fleet young and modern. This has been made possible by a strong cash flow that has allowed the airline to maintain a fuel-efficient fleet averaging just over five years of age, without resorting to heavy borrowing or costly leasing deals. The fleets of most other international carriers are more than twice as old as SIA's. While this strategy entails heavy capital costs, it translates into significant savings through minimising aircraft downtime and maintenance costs. Newer aircraft are also faster and more fuel efficient, and are perceived by passengers to be safer.

SIA's strategy can therefore be described as one of steady growth, and of taking the long-term strategic view. It does not simply react to cyclical and transient market conditions. It invests in capacity and increases route frequency only when it is confident that there is a market for it. This means that operations are not necessarily cut back when yields indicate a downward trend or when a particular business is struggling during its start-up or infancy stage. SIA is also well governed and managed. Every sector of the business is monitored and managed at the "macro" level as well as the "micro" level. Comprehensive reporting flows through the company as a matter of routine. Problems or issues are investigated and examined expeditiously. For example, if there is a decline in market share, it would check out a competitor's aggressive fare discounting or a change in the popularity of flight patterns. SIA also runs an ongoing program of cost cutting, and every two years it conducts a Towards Optimal Productivity program, which reviews the way the company operates and finds ways to do things better.

From a brand perspective, this story has all the elements of a "best seller". It combines the vision necessary to create a great brand with the brand values necessary to satisfy the customer's needs, and with a willingness of heart to sustain delivery. There were probably several hundred ice-creams on ice in the galley. But my "friend" the purser, went to great lengths to make me believe that not only was I the most important customer on that plane, but that I would leave the flight determined to return, and equally determined to tell a few thousand friends. Well sir, the only thing we need to do now is sell a few thousand copies of this book.

Section 2
Understanding Your Brand

10
Defining your business

You'll have concluded by now that we don't believe in reinventing the wheel. There have been a vast number of learned and savvy business analysts and consultants who have given the world a great deal of insight and guidance, not just about brands, but about business strategy in general. We have unashamedly quoted from some of the best because they have said what they have to say, better than anyone else ever could.

We introduced Theodore Levitt as the man who first pondered the difference between marketing and selling, and agreed with his conclusion that selling focuses on the needs of the seller while marketing looks at the needs of the buyer. Levitt's insight reinforces the critical need to understand your customer. In support of Levitt, we quoted Drucker's famous line, that without a customer you don't have a business. We don't resile from either of those principles, but for the moment we want to put them to one side and make another conclusive statement.

If you can't define something, you can't sell it.

We're not exactly sure who actually said it first, or whether that's the original quote, but the reality behind the statement is absolute gold.

- If you review any reference book on strategic planning you will be confronted by a number of unavoidable steps that must be taken before you can get to the detail of business planning. The first is to create a mission statement. Your mission will typically contain three parts: a corporate vision, which describes how the management team sees the business in the future; a business definition, which describes your targets, your customers' needs and the key competitive advantage of the business; and thirdly, a list of values that need to be in place for the business to succeed.

Sound familiar? Of course it does, because the similarities between strategic planning and brand planning are unavoidable. However, experience has shown us that there is a fundamental mistake companies make in their strategic planning exercises and it comes in two parts. First, many companies struggle, and often fail, to correctly identify the industry in which they operate. Then they compound the problem by not clearly defining their business. And the reasons are very simple: These companies only pay lip service to the customer's needs and fail to look beyond the predictable environment of their product.

Part of the answer lies in something Theodore Levitt talked about half a century ago.

In 1960 Ted Levitt penned for the *Harvard Business Review* a short article that has since become a marketing classic and one of the publication's most widely quoted and anthologised pieces; it is constantly recycled by marketing lecturers and tutors around the world. In fact, the *Harvard Business Review* has sold in excess of a quarter of a million copies of the article, entitled "Marketing Myopia". In the article, Levitt reflected on the way short-sighted managements often fail to see their business in light of growth opportunities, and too narrowly define what their business actually does.

In "Marketing Myopia", Levitt urged businesses to define their industries outside of the predictable square, to take advantage of not only growth, but also change. He used the example of the US railways and showed how they had declined as technology advanced, because they defined themselves too narrowly.

Levitt's claim was that the railways did not stop growing because the need for passenger and freight transportation declined. In fact, that grew exponentially. Nor did the railways stop growing because the need was filled by other modes such as cars, trucks and aeroplanes. The answer, Levitt argued, was that the railways stopped growing because they didn't fill the need themselves. Levitt criticised the railways for failing to look beyond existing boundaries:

They let others take customers away from them because they assumed themselves to be in the railroad business rather than in the transportation business.[22]

Essentially, Levitt was arguing that companies could only expect to continue growing if they understood and acted on their customers' needs and desires, and did not simply rely on the presumed longevity of their products.

He postulated that every major industry was once a growth industry, and that their decline was not because the market became saturated; rather, in each case, there was a failure to understand the business by those at the very top of the organisation responsible for its broad aims and policies (in other words, the strategic plan).

The railways allowed other modes of transport to take their customers away from them because they defined their industry as railway oriented instead of transport oriented. Or, in other words, they were product oriented, not customer oriented.

Think about the railway business for a moment. The problem with railways is that they are limited by where their transport can go. Once you run out of rail, that's the end of you. However, people's needs don't run out when the track does. If you're living even two kilometres from the railway station there is still a transport gap that has to be filled.

If someone asks you what business you are in, how do you reply? Think first about the industry you are part of, and the need you fulfil in that industry. Then think about it from the perspective of your customers and what they need.

If a company spends hundreds of thousands of dollars to buy equipment that will roll and shape steel and aluminium, what business are they in? When we asked the senior management of this particular company they said they were in the business of bending steel. We disagreed with them, and argued that they were in the business of building better bridges, or providing solutions for manufacturers to create cost efficiencies.

One of the examples Levitt uses in "Marketing Myopia" is the different insight that evolved in Hollywood following the introduction of television. The television executives made no bones about it; they were in the entertainment business. Unfortunately the Hollywood movie moguls who succeeded the likes of Adolph Zukor, naively believed they were still in the business of making movies. Consider the critical difference: if you're in the movie-making business, what you are accepting is a specific, limited product — you make movies. If you're in the entertainment business you are constantly looking for ways to ensure that you can entertain your customers. The movie moguls scorned and rejected TV when, in fact, they should have embraced the opportunity of broader entertainment provided under the auspices of the new medium, or for that matter, any new medium, even those that hadn't been invented at the time. From an industry perspective, Hollywood was product focused, rather than customer focused. It will be intriguing to see the shape of the industry in 20 years and whether the executives of today have been clever enough to understand how their industry is changing.

The English Football Association (FA) would not be offering the world the best brand of club football if they had remained, as they were in the 1960s, just a football association. Liverpool, Chelsea, Tottenham Hotspur, Arsenal and Manchester United are names that are recognised around the world for much more than just football. Why? Because they are well and truly entrenched in the entertainment business — not the sport business, and definitely not the football business.

The English FA recognised decades ago where it needed to be to compete on a world stage for the hearts and minds of its fans. It set about making the game pure entertainment and that meant buying the best, and showing the best. To accommodate, FA had to change the way it went about its business. It openly encouraged entrepreneurs from Russia who had made billions from oil to "own" a team. Even another country's ex-prime minister, a man accused of corruption by his own government, was allowed to purchase a franchise. Television viewing rights were the lynchpin and the money started to flow. Everywhere you go in the world you will find English football: a hotel room in Bangkok; a private home in Mumbai; an apartment in Paris; or a penthouse in San Francisco. It competes against the best entertainment on offer, and although the business model has been cloned by other associations, it is unlikely that they will ever take away the number one mantle — unless of course the English FA reverts to just being a game played with a round ball and two teams of eleven players.

Newspaper owners who think they are in the newsprint game deserve to be out of a job. Just over a decade ago that is exactly how some of the world's greatest press barons saw themselves. The clever ones, those still in business, such as Rupert Murdoch, saw themselves in the information industry, and adapted accordingly, realising that their customers would soon be getting big slabs of their information from non-traditional providers.

As we write this book, Murdoch has thrown out possibly the biggest challenge of his career to one of the world's newest but largest brands: Google. Murdoch has called for Google and other major search engines and online news purveyors to pay for his material, the stories and articles written by Murdoch journalists around the world. When you read this, you may already know the outcome of this challenge. If Murdoch won, he will no doubt have celebrated his decision to operate in a much bigger game than the newspaper business. If he lost — we still believe he had little choice.

Read the financial pages of a newspaper and see how many other companies are succumbing to the same failures as the misguided newspaper owners. If you want further inspiration, go back to Levitt. He pointed to the dry cleaning industry as one that promised its lucky members huge wealth and success. Then along came synthetics and blew some very serious holes in profit and loss sheets. The problems didn't arise because someone invented a better way of cleaning, but through the failure of managements to define what business they were in. Equally, energy companies can't afford to be suppliers of electricity, and the telcos would have failed to survive if they had stuck with cables or fixed line communication.

So what industry are you working in? Is it the newspaper business or the communications business? Perhaps you see it as the metal bending business, as opposed to the building and fabrication industry? Perhaps we're being a little harsh in our criticism of Adolph Zukor; after all, he had the wisdom to build a theatrical chain of over 2000 outlets to show his movies. But, ask yourself the hard question: Was Zukor thinking outside the square from an industry perspective, or did he simply tie up distribution to his own advantage?

The distinction is telling, and sets up the next chapter. But be aware, if you haven't understood the key message from this chapter, the need to define the 'real' business you are in, frankly, you're wasting your time even turning the page.

11
Drill bits versus holes

Are you focused on products or needs? That's the most important question you should be considering at the moment. Do you believe that people buy the drill bit because they need a long piece of metal, or because it is the most convenient tool to get the hole they actually need? Put that way, the answer is pretty obvious and almost insulting to ask, but from experience we know that many executives struggle with the concept of *"customer needs"* and how it works in their business.

The starting point to becoming customer focused in any business is to undertake a *brand analysis* as outlined in Chapter Five, paying particular attention to the transition of attributes into benefits.

In a large organisation the brand analysis would be undertaken in a workshop attended by a number of senior executives, representing all the key disciplines from within the company. They should include the Chief Executive Officer, the Chief Financial Officer, the Human Resource Manager, the senior IT person and of course the Marketing Manager. In a smaller organisation attendance is dictated by best fit, and if you're a sole trader, sit down and get comfortable with the white board.

The first question most participants ask during the workshop is: What do you mean by *attributes?* To adequately answer the question requires us to step back and consider the decisions relating to the development and marketing of individual products.

The most fundamental attribute of any product or service is quality. Quality involves a range of factors such as durability, reliability, ease of operation and so on. And it is the primary determinant of price, looks and appeal, depending on where it is positioned on the quality continuum, from the very pinnacle to the very nadir. Quality is a deliberate decision taken by the purveyor of the product or service and becomes a key part of how a product is positioned.

Other attributes are perhaps not quite as obvious, and the workshop participants sometimes struggle to see beyond quality. They need a starting point for the discussion and the simplest place to begin is with the *features* of their product or service. While this means adding a third dimension to the process, it provides a sound platform to assess the potential *attributes,* before translating those attributes into possible *benefits.*

When developing a product or service most people use the term "feature" to define the parts that make up the whole. An examination of the features then enables them to define the potential points of difference between their product and that of their competition. To all intents and purposes an "attribute" can be described in the same way, but with one significant difference. Unlike a feature, an attribute has the capacity to define a benefit because it can be a rational and emotional characteristic, while a feature can only ever be an objective statement of fact. And in the business of brands, emotion plays a critical role.

The dictionary definitions of features and attributes helps put this into context. "Feature" is defined as *"a prominent or conspicuous part or characteristic"*, while the definition of "attribute" talks about *"something attributed as belonging; a quality, character, characteristic or property"*. The difference is highlighted in this example: Medical knowledge is a required feature of all doctors; wisdom is an attribute of only some.

So, how do those definitions help us to understand or identify the benefits?

By definition, the answer is fairly straightforward; in practice, the process is not quite as simple. A *benefit* is what the attribute is interpreted to be when you ask the WIFM, or *'What's in it for me?'* question. In the doctor scenario, the benefit is *better health through better diagnosis*, assured by the doctor's wisdom. What we are seeking is the one reason, or cluster of reasons that will make a real difference to the customer.

Product features are well illustrated through the pages of the glossy brochures used by car manufacturers to sell their wares. Turn to the last couple of pages of one such brochure and you'll find them listed, often in dot point form, or in a series of columns showing which features are available on what model. The list of features is endless: ABS brakes; tinted windscreen (if the laws in your country allow such a luxury); and a range of colours, generally one green, one blue, one red, one white, one black, all available in metallic paint at an additional (and not insignificant) cost. Of course there is an engine with ever-improving energy efficiencies, a radio and an air conditioner. There could also be a DVD player in the back for the kids and a GPS in the front for the big kids.

But is any one or combination of these features the reason someone buys a car?

Or chooses a Mont Blanc pen instead of a Parker?

Of course, the answer is both yes, and no.

This is where the matter of features becomes complex. A rational feature of a pen is blue, black or red ink; another is the clip that secures the pen inside your jacket; while another is the thickness of the nib or ball. But regardless of how good these features are, they do not immediately translate into benefits from the *'What's in it for me?'* perspective.

What becomes apparent in the workshop environment is that some features translate into powerful benefits because they are much stronger attributes, even though other features are still intrinsic to the question of WIFM, without necessarily being the driver. Some features don't even get a ranking. The difficulty is differentiating between them.

A feature of a vineyard may be that old oak vats are used to mature the wine; the attribute is the flavour facilitated by the oak vats. A feature of a hotel may be that it is the tallest building in the city; the attribute is a spectacular view. A feature of a painting may be that it is framed using non-reflective glass; the attribute is a clear view of the subject.

So that gives us two parts of the equation. We can identify the features of a product or service, and with some lateral thinking, identify which of the features have attributes worth pursuing as benefits. How do we take that final step?

Consider this statement made nearly 40 years ago by Charles Revlon, the man behind one of the most famous cosmetic houses in the world. Revlon was talking to a group of colleagues about the company's lipstick products when he made the following remark:

When it leaves the factory, it's lipstick, but when it reaches the department store, it's hope.

We defy anyone to express the concept of WIFM any more succinctly.

We deliberately chose the pen and the car as our examples to demonstrate the point that regardless of the number of features you can list, the sum total of that list is not necessarily the reason you will purchase that particular car, or that particular pen. They will certainly contribute to that decision, but in both cases, and among a range of prospects, each purchaser will unconsciously prioritise different features.

They will be helped in that process by the presentation of material, and of course, by their own preferences and emotions. Throughout the car manufacturer's brochure the car's features are pictorially translated into an emotional statement in exquisite photographs that someone has spent hours lighting to perfection.

The colour of the ink is, on the surface, a fairly straightforward and expected feature of a pen, regardless of the brand. But the colour of the ink is also an emotional attribute. Some people will only ever sign their name with black ink; in fact, black is stipulated on some legal documents including tax forms. Equally, the ribbed design feature on the side of the casing may make you feel more comfortable holding it, and while some people prefer the feel of a thick nib when they write, others may well prefer their pen strokes to be light and easy flowing.

The decision to buy the car will be made long before the colour is chosen, or before it is established whether the vehicle has ABS brakes. And although the purchase decision on the pen will not be quite as complex, nevertheless, it is unlikely to come down to one or more features. So what is the *Revlon analogy* for your business? How can we turn lipstick into "hope"?

You can begin by undertaking the following simple exercise.

Down the left-hand side of a blank piece of paper, list what you consider to be the attributes of your business or product. If you still feel uncomfortable about defining them as attributes, list them as features, but be careful to consider every feature, regardless of how important or unimportant you think it might be. You can get a guide to this by referring to the car brochure, or any retail advertisement comparing one air-conditioning unit to another, or two different branded wide-screen televisions. Chances are the advertisement will list the major selling features.

If you run a service organisation the list might not be quite as straightforward, so let's consider how a list of attributes for a travel agency might look.

- Wide range of the latest holiday packages
- Competitive pricing
- Knowledgeable and experienced consultants
- Current computer hardware and software
- Knowledge of regulatory requirements
- Credit card facilities
- Strong point of sale

The actual list is probably longer, but for the moment, this will suffice. Now, on the right-hand side of your sheet of paper, translate the attributes you've listed into a customer benefit, from the perspective of the customer, naturally.

Simple, right? Well, actually, no, not quite so simple. The truth of the matter is very few people automatically view things from the customer's perspective.

12

Six hats or one?

Edward De Bono suggested we use six hats to understand what makes our customers tick. In his book, *Six Thinking Hats*, De Bono develops a methodology to expand the ultimate human resource, the one absolute that sets the human race apart from every other species: our capacity to think. De Bono's proposition is to remove the complexity and confusion from the thinking process. He explains his premise in the preface to his book:

The main difficulty of thinking is confusion. We try to do too much at once. Emotions, information, logic, hope and creativity all crowd in on us. It is like juggling with too many balls.

Dr De Bono is widely regarded as the leading authority in the direct teaching of thinking as a skill. He has held faculty appointments at some of the best known university brands, including Oxford, Cambridge and Harvard, and has addressed leading business executives, presidents, prime ministers and students in over 50 countries around the world. He even has a planet named after him. De Bono originated the concept of lateral thinking and contributed to our understanding of the brain as a self-organising system. His *six hats* provide a creative thinking tool to tackle any problem through constructive process rather than adversarial argument, allowing the user to view the debate from six different perspectives.

We have used De Bono's *six hats* to develop advertising strategy with fantastic results. Each of the hats becomes a thinking mode: blue sets the agenda and acts as the chair; white guides our information needs, what we know, what we need to know; black forces us to look at the negatives; yellow helps us to look at the positives; red provides us with both the raw emotion and the gut feel; and finally, green gives us the opportunity to look for, and examine alternatives.

What De Bono's *six hats* empower us to do is to think strategically and logically. However, as fascinating and clever as De Bono's lateral thinking processes are, they still don't resolve how we get *inside* our customers' heads, and think like them.

In each case we really only need one hat, the customer's, but we need to wear it in such a way that we are able to think like the customer, and that, unfortunately, doesn't always mean to think logically. In this endeavour we have only one desired outcome: to get inside the heads of our customers in such a way that we can see what we need to, from their perspective.

The way to do that requires an understanding of three aligned and interacting factors, the first of which is the all-pervasive nature of brands.

We are surrounded by brands. We've already explored what can become a brand and the list is endless. Not just predictable commodity items such as breakfast cereals, washing powders or motor cars. There are brands in every corner of the home, and you encounter them in every moment of your day. Even if you're watching the six o'clock news and questioning whether the world should respond to Kim Jong-Il's ongoing nuclear threat, well, like it or not, you're dealing with a brand. Barack Obama and the redoubtable Kim Jong-Il are both brands, and your mind and your judgement is dealing with these types of brands every minute of every day.

The second factor is that brands are an integral part of our behaviour patterns; behaviour is based on beliefs, and when you combine a particular set of beliefs it usually triggers a certain action. On just about every occasion that action involves a brand.

The third factor is the inevitability of changing behaviour and the impact that has on brands.

Put simply, unless you can actually alter a person's beliefs, you can't change his or her behaviour. So if you want to change a person's attitude towards your brand, you have to understand his or her current beliefs about your product or service category. The final part of the process is to determine how important three things are in the hierarchy of beliefs in the person's mind: the overall category, the person's current brand choice in that category, and your brand.

Inside every one of us is a complex network of hundreds of thousands of interconnected beliefs. Some are core beliefs, the very essence of your character and morality; God, country and your football team probably get equal billing in this category.

At the other end of the scale are your non-core beliefs such as your love of, or dislike for your prime minister or president. These beliefs may be as low on your importance scale as that bestowed by most people on real estate agents, advertising practitioners and journalists.

Also down there with the non-core or low order beliefs is your favourite brand of soft drink, your preferred coffee or the cereal you prefer for breakfast.

Higher up the scale, heading closer to your core beliefs, are those weighted with greater importance: the new car you intend to buy; or whether you should be seen in this year's fashion, or last year's hardly worn, but sadly dated, elegant cocktail dress.

In this hierarchy, some are rational, highly practical beliefs, while others are unashamedly emotional. Equally, some are very conscious, in-your-face beliefs. Others are hidden away in your subconscious and only rarely sighted.

Of even greater import, is that some of these beliefs are true, while unfortunately, many others are not. And even more unfortunate, is that many of the beliefs that are not factual are actually believed to be so, by the person involved.

Such a convoluted hierarchical belief system must come from somewhere. These hundreds of thousands of beliefs didn't just rise out of the dust.

The simple fact is that every one of these beliefs came from some form of communication.

When you were a child, your mother and father probably spent hundreds of hours instructing you on what was right and wrong. Then your teachers — including your Sunday school or other religious teacher, if you had one — added another layer to your belief system, aided by your school friends, your neighbours, not to mention your brothers and sisters.

What makes this an intriguing proposition is that what your parents taught you, and what your teachers taught you, and what you heard from everyone else around you, all went in the same ear, and all finished up in the same brain. There, this information swirled around, one idea trying to make sense of another.

Your eyes and ears weren't the only appendages to transmit information to your brain. At 12 years of age, Gorgonzola cheese smelt worse than your footy socks or netball uniform. By the time you'd reached 35, it was the only acceptable smell to complement a rich, tawny port.

Taste and touch came into it as well. Imagine the disappointment of discovering sex without the added bonus of taste and touch.

From the very earliest age we have been taking beliefs on board. And with each new belief, our system has been forced to establish its own hierarchy of importance. Nothing is more important to a small baby than the taste, smell and feel of its mother's breast. By the age of three that belief has slipped in the rankings to be replaced by another form of food, or even something other than food entirely. And as the child grows, the hierarchy becomes more complex. Beliefs crowd in on top of beliefs. New beliefs fight with existing beliefs. The hierarchy constantly changes. What was important yesterday might become less so the day after.

The older we are, the more we challenge new beliefs and the more protective we are of existing beliefs. Each year seems to add a layer of cynicism and scepticism. New beliefs find it harder to shift more entrenched beliefs and similar beliefs are rejected because they don't offer something new. The brain becomes a swirling mass of shifting and moving beliefs that become increasingly difficult to change or alter.

Into this cauldron we pitch brand after brand, product after product. And the marketers presume that their brand, their carefully, diligently executed brand will not only survive in this environment, it will outshine every other brand.

Then the marketers become depressed when the targets, who they so carefully identified, reject their brand or worse, ignore it altogether. Being ignored is an even greater insult to their brand than rejection.

Yet, how could we possibly expect anything else to happen? How could we possibly expect a new brand to assume greater importance in this hierarchy than the competitive brand, which has been a part of the target's belief system for a decade?

"Because our brand is better," the marketers will say. "Because our brand has significant improvements over the competition," they add.

Well, frankly, if a brand gets caught up in the beliefs minefield and doesn't receive proper care and attention there's every chance that it will get chewed up and spat out before it even gets a chance to cut it as a brand. Believing that it's a better brand won't help. Actually knowing it's a better brand won't help either. And just to add to the mayhem, the minefield has been growing larger and larger with each passing year.

So how do we cut through the maze if De Bono's *six hats* aren't going to help?

13

What would your customers know?

Advertising strategy is probably the closest thing to brand strategy and the 'What's in it for me?' principle. Every advertising agency worth its socks has its own strategic thinking process. In the end, each process comes down to a simple understanding of what the target *currently thinks about 'your' brand*, (or doesn't, as the case may be), and how *you want them to think* after they have been exposed to your brand.

The once powerful advertising agency, Ogilvy & Mather, encouraged its strategists to write briefs in the 'first person' as a member of the target audience, a practice that forced the people writing the ads to think like the target they were intending to talk to.

Good strategy development insists that we think of the intention to shift behaviour in terms of one person, not a group.

The marketing objective might require an increase of 30 per cent in turnover. The objective of the advertising might be more specific: get the person who eats at Five Guys Burgers &

Fries twice a year to eat there six times a year. The question we need to answer is: How do we unlock the individual's belief system or alter the person's WIFM perspective to achieve the results?

Once again the answer appears simple but the reality may not be. If you want to persuade a person to go to Five Guys Burgers & Fries six times a year instead of twice, you have to understand the beliefs that are currently stopping that person from making the extra four trips.

Focusing on one person does not preclude others from being persuaded to think this way. But by thinking of only one person we get the advertising writer into the habit of visualising one person making the switch, or changing behaviour. That also means thinking in terms beyond demographics. If our advertising writer only thinks of the target in one-dimensional demographic terms it's very hard to get inside that person's head. But if our writer visualises one person, the writer can actually 'talk' to that person. The writer can imagine sitting down with the target and exploring the concerns and belief patterns that make that person think of a brand in a certain way.

Good brand communication is about creating, altering or intensifying a target's beliefs in such a way that it will have a positive impact on your product or service. It may be as clear cut as getting them to buy something. Equally it may be about shifting a belief a part of the way to accepting the new or changed belief and, thereby, the new behaviour.

But how do we obtain the information we need to help the writer pursue the conversation he or she needs to have with the target? Unfortunately, our belief system does not work in a rational *six hats* kind of way. There is no logical pattern for thoughts to come forward in the subconscious. There is no regulated order of things, and even though you can compartmentalise some of the decision-making process, you will never succeed in getting it into any logical order or sequence.

Many business executives, managers and owners fail to see this truth because they fail to see the customer's point of view. They prefer to trust the repetitive sales transactions, without digging deeper. If they did, what would they find? Often people will remain loyal on the surface, because there is nowhere else to go. The US railways discovered that, to their peril. Repeat purchase that is reliant on a monopoly is open to exploitation as soon as someone comes up with a better offering.

Large banks reinforce this premise by failing to see the customer's point of view. A recent survey conducted by Roy Morgan Research, Australia's largest independent research company, showed that almost one-third of bank customers are unhappy with the service they receive from their banks, in particular the big four banks. Small business owners were even more critical, with one of the banks, NAB, receiving only 55.6 per cent customer satisfaction. The winners were the smaller banks, and the building societies and credit unions, which achieved customer satisfaction ratings in excess of 85 per cent of customers.

Do the bank executives deliberately bury their heads in the sand? In a media release from Roy Morgan, the company's CEO opined that the major banks were still not meeting the needs of their small business customers and that the major reason to switch banks is because the big banks simply "don't care about loyal customers".

In fact we suspect that the reason more customers don't switch is because it is simply 'too hard' to do so, and the major banks understand and exploit this.

Other managers display what we will call organisational arrogance: they assume they know what customers want, or what's best for them.

We suspect that the major hotels were guilty of this for years. On the surface they appeared to be listening to their customers. Every five star hotel would leave a satisfaction survey in their rooms for customers to fill out. In actual fact only a very small percentage of customers do so, and generally they are customers happy with the hotel. (Those unhappy with the hotel respond with their feet — they don't come back.)

This means the satisfaction ratings are usually high, certainly above 90 per cent, and although five star hotels are diligent in maintaining their standards so they don't lose customers, these types of surveys do little in providing customer insight.

Next time you stay in a quality hotel, look around and take a note of the features of the room. Then consider how many of the features you actually use. When you're travelling on business, do you really use the DVD player? When was the last time you used the bedside alarm to wake you up in the morning (as opposed to using your mobile, or a wake-up call)? Probably the first thing you do when staying in a hotel on business is plug your computer in to check emails. Does it annoy you when you discover that the connection process takes longer than the check-in process downstairs did, and you're going to be paying $20 for the privilege?

The one thing travellers today look for is an iron and an ironing board to resolve the problem of bad packing techniques.

It really isn't that long ago that most five star hotels didn't provide this equipment because pressing clothes was a revenue earner. Please note we deliberately have avoided calling this a service.

If we go back far enough it's probably fair to say that more than 50 per cent of hotel guests wouldn't actually know how to use an iron, but that is not the case today. Now, if the hotel really wants to provide a 'service', it provides the iron and the ironing board, not a so-called service that costs money for something you can do yourself. Some hotels have also seen the light in regard to internet connections and provide the service free (at very little cost to the hotel). We wonder how long it will be before all hotels are listening to their customers in this regard.

Research for a training organisation undertaken by a colleague showed that after enrolling in a training course customers were comfortable with a response time of five days to receive their registration papers through the mail. Even after the research findings were presented the organisation in question continued to apply pressure on staff to turn the registration papers around in three days. Why? Because the management believed it was important.

Surely the smart thing to have done would be to listen to your customers, set in place the less onerous system of turning the material around within the week and then apply the available resources where they really would change attitudes or opinions.

Most managers use market research in the first instance to determine whether there is a market need for their service or product. Although they base their research on a hypothesis, the outcome will be more about the answer they want to hear, rather than the one they need to hear. They will ultimately match customers with products or services but will have achieved no better an outcome than those managers who bury their heads in the sand or the others who suffer from organisational arrogance.

The type of research we're criticising asks questions that provide little insight into why customers make certain decisions; they simply reinforce the manager's desired position. Instead of asking questions that dare to pose the *why* question, and may possibly reveal the WIFM perspective, they ask questions such as: *Which product would you choose, a, b, or c?* Or, *which package is most attractive to you?* And they finish up with an answer that is superficial and one-dimensional.

Unfortunately, those higher up the hierarchy know even less about market research than these managers do, and simply nod their heads sagely when presented with data showing that 95 per cent of respondents overwhelmingly preferred option b.

We shake our heads, and wonder why.

When asked by a direct debit company to review a new product aimed at a particular market segment, a research colleague prepared a questionnaire that asked nothing about the product in the first half dozen questions. The client was alarmed and wanted to know why. The response was quite simple: because we know nothing about the target except for anecdotal information. We don't know what alternatives the target currently uses (instead of the proposed product), the environment in which the target operates, or why the target does things in a certain way. At the end of the day, the target customer might actually be happier without some newfangled product.

Most hotels, airlines and other large service groups (such as universities) use their satisfaction surveys as measures, rather than customer insight. But even that distinction presumes that they have the insight in the first place.

In all the research we do, the fundamental question we want answered is the WIFM question. By asking which package a customer likes we can refine the package, but we do so without the insight that it is actually important to the customer.

So how do you get inside your customers' heads and understand their WIFM perspective? Part of the answer is in the questions you ask. The other part is in how you ask them.

Now, at this point we need to pause and make an observation that will hopefully remove any scent or suggestion of plagiarism. In the 1980s and 90s there were many consultants who got very rich selling quality management systems. In their wisdom they quoted chapter and verse from marketing text books. They advocated the principles of brands without ever mentioning the word 'brand'. They also borrowed very heavily from market research text books and practitioners. One such consultant was Karl Albrecht who wrote several books on the subject. We first became aware of Albrecht in the late 80s following publication of his book, *Service America*. We know of several senior executives in the advertising game who handed copies out to their management teams, urging them to read a different view on the premise of brands. Many of the beliefs we are espousing in this book mirror the principles of quality management because the ultimate proof of a successful brand is in repeat purchase, and the ultimate way to ensure that occurs is through quality and consistency.

If you studied psychology you will be very familiar with Maslow's hierarchy of needs.[25]

Albrecht applied a similar principle to what he called the hierarchy of customer value.

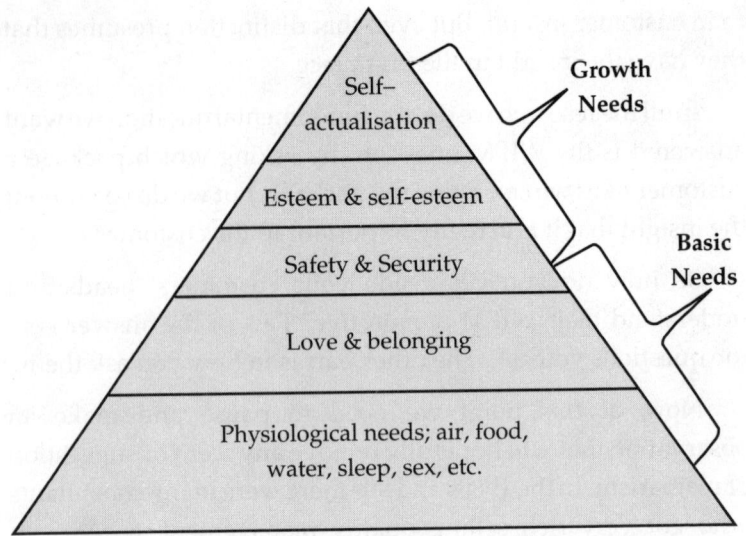

Maslow's Hierarchy of Needs

Maslow has set up a hierarchy of five levels of basic needs. Beyond these needs, higher levels of needs exist. These include needs for understanding, aesthetic appreciation and purely spiritual needs. In the levels of the five basic needs, the person does not feel the second need until the demands of the first have been satisfied; or the third until the second has been satisfied, and so on.

Maslow's basic needs:

Physiological Needs

These are biological needs. They consist of needs for oxygen, food, water, and a relatively constant body temperature. They are the strongest needs because if a person were deprived of all needs, the physiological ones would come first in the person's search for satisfaction.

Safety Needs

When all physiological needs are satisfied and are no longer controlling thoughts and behaviours, the needs for security can become active. Adults have little awareness of their security needs except in times of emergency or periods of disorganisation in the social structure (such as widespread rioting). Children often display the signs of insecurity and the need to be safe.

Needs of Love, Affection and Belongingness

When the needs for safety and for physiological well-being are satisfied, the next class of needs, for love, affection and belongingness, can emerge. Maslow states that people seek to overcome feelings of loneliness and alienation. This involves both giving and receiving love, affection and the sense of belonging.

Needs for Esteem

When the first three classes of needs are satisfied, the needs for esteem can become dominant. These involve needs for both self-esteem and for the esteem a person gets from others. Humans have a need for a stable, firmly based, high level of self-respect, and respect from others. When these needs are satisfied, the person feels self-confident and valuable in the world. When these needs are frustrated, the person feels inferior, weak, helpless and worthless.

Needs for Self-Actualisation

When all of the other needs are satisfied, then and only then, are the needs for self-actualisation activated. Maslow describes self-actualisation as a person's need to be and do that which the person was "born to do". "A musician must make music, an artist must paint, and a poet must write."

> These needs make themselves felt in signs of restlessness. The person feels on-edge, tense, lacking something, in short, restless. If a person is hungry, unsafe, not loved or accepted, or lacking self-esteem, it is very easy to know what the person is restless about. It is not always clear what a person wants when there is a need for self-actualisation.

The beliefs system that we discussed in the previous chapter suggests a much more random genesis than Maslow's hierarchy. Fortunately, our contention that it is extraordinarily complex is, in part, redeemed by some fundamental questions that you can ask to move along the pathway to understanding the customer's WIFM perspective of your product or service.

Albrecht designed a customer value hierarchy with four levels, which is perhaps not as contentious as Maslow's theory and may help us establish our WIFM hierarchy. Albrecht contended that there were a number of absolutely basic attributes, either tangible or intangible, and without them there is no point going to the next stage. Let's call these the

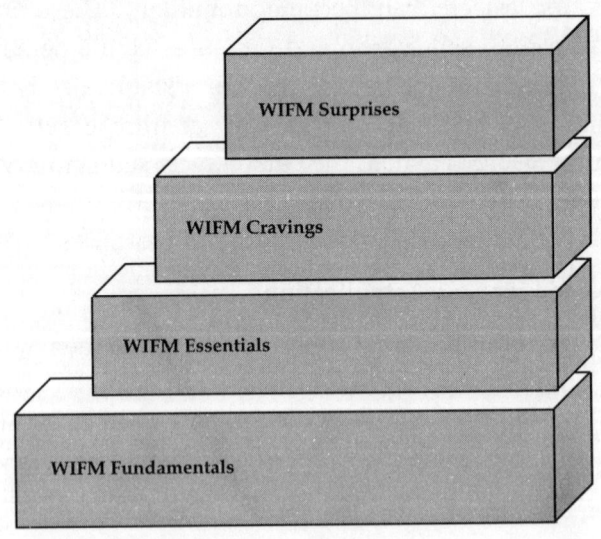

WIFM Fundamentals: the supermarket aisles are stocked with food; the electrical appliance has a plug and cord as standard; the water in the bottle is clean and the bottle is sealed; and the airline has planes, and the coffee contains beans.

The next level, according to Albrecht, contains the expected attributes — those that customers take for granted as part of their expectation of the generic product or service group. Let's call them the *WIFM Essentials:* the supermarket will have assistants at the check-out; the electrical appliance will perform the task it is designed for, better than the customer's previous appliance; the water in the bottle comes from a spring, not the tap;and the airline has a good safety record and the coffee is fresh.

Next, Albrecht identified desired attributes, those the customer doesn't expect, but hopes the product or service has. We will call them the *WIFM Cravings:* the supermarket assistants will smile at you and wish you a good day; the electrical appliance switches itself off to save energy; the water actually tastes like it came from a spring; and the airline seats have more space than usual and the coffee aroma is out of this world.

Finally, Albrecht described the fourth layer or tier of attributes as the unanticipated: those attributes that go beyond the customer's desires or expectations. We are going to call them *WIFM Surprises:* the supermarket assistant offers to carry your bags to the car; a letter arrives from the appliance manufacturer, personally signed by the CEO and giving you the direct line in case something goes wrong; the water comes with a pledge by the company's CEO to channel all profit into supporting climate change; and the flight attendant tells you that your seat is double-booked, asks if you would mind sitting in business class, and the coffee tastes as good as it smells.

Consider how you would apply the WIFM hierarchy to your business.

What are the *WIFM Fundamentals* and *Essentials* about your product or service? Which attributes must you perform well on to be worthy of a place in the market? These are the absolute basics expected of your business. You learn these fundamentals through experience in your industry. You don't have to be Einstein to understand them but you must get them right if you are to even consider competing.

Your point of difference emerges when you start to progress beyond these levels. This is where your competitive edge begins to take shape. If you only do the basics, regardless of how well you do them, customers will most likely see you as ordinary, unless of course this is the level your competitors are at.

If you fulfil the *fundamentals, essentials* and *cravings* well, your customers will start to favour you over your competitors — particularly if you do them better than your competitors.

Of course, if you *surprise* the customer, then you should be streets in front of your competitors. Gail Kelly, CEO of Westpac Bank, has an aspiration to "delight customers". Kelly is known to personally answer customer complaints, and was named the 18th most powerful woman in the world by *Forbes* business magazine, "outranking US first lady Michelle Obama, Hillary Clinton, talk show queen Oprah Winfrey and even real royalty, her majesty the Queen."[26]

But quality management is only part of the story, and once again, this is where the power of brand thinking comes into its own to make sure that you can constantly *surprise* your customer.

14

We are talking about emotional ownership

There is an inescapable fact about brands that quality management systems cannot adequately define or capture, and it is this: The essence of brand thinking is in the emotional connection that gives the customer control over the purchase decision. Remember, you don't own your own brand, the customer does!

You can't change that simple premise but you can harness its power to build your success.

Many managers struggle to understand the structure of the relationship between their product or service and their customers, which we defined in Chapter Two:

Consumers perceive the value of a "branded" product or service to be greater than the sum of its tangible assets. We can't always define the intangible aspects as accurately as we would wish because it is so individual and personal to each consumer; but this is where the promise of a brand, and the true power of a brand, begins to emerge. Brands build relationships. In fact, the brand is the very essence of the relationship built between the consumer and the product or service for sale. And relationships are the very cornerstone of success for any business because they represent repeat business.

We concluded that managing the image of a product or service, so that it creates a desirable identity greater than the sum of its parts, should be the ultimate goal of anyone wanting to create a brand. Your aim must be to create a brand which, first and foremost, meets the consumer's 'What's in it for me?' expectation; that the consumer can relate to; and last, but most important of all, a brand the consumer wants to purchase repeatedly, and indeed recommend to others.

Most decisions taken to stop using a product or service are emotional, not physical or pragmatic, which means you must constantly be wary of the subjective, rather than the objective.

The world of brands is about repeat purchase, but this is underpinned by the recognition that what the customer gives, only the customer can take away. Of course this is contrary to all we learn when we are at school or at our parent's knee. We are taught to equate value to the objective and quantifiable characteristics of tangible products. Even when we discuss desirable features in a product or service we are almost always dealing with a measurable or quantifiable characteristic. The car advertisement details the performance characteristics, and the manufacturer promotes the fact that the jumper is made of wool and won't shrink, or the soft drink doesn't contain sugar. These are measurable, observable and, therefore, quantifiable characteristics. All of our training and traditional thinking is based on a definition of quality as an objective, intrinsic characteristic of something tangible. Even in the business of education or training the tangible outcome is the piece of paper that represents our qualification.

This is the tangible versus the intangible; the pragmatic versus the emotional. For whatever reason, good or bad, emotions and emotional connections are not the stuff of most of our conversations. Try to explain an intangible to someone and you will probably finish up tongue-tied. Fortunately for the modern world there are a burgeoning number of fiction authors who help us in our endeavour to explore the emotional world.

But can we afford to let it remain the stuff of fiction? Equally, do we have the persuasive ability to make it sit just as comfortably in the pragmatic world of the board room?

On a recent holiday to India a colleague arranged all his accommodation and travel arrangements though an agent in Delhi. The agent had been recommended and the package submitted was cost-friendly and covered all the things that had been requested. There had been a number of email exchanges during negotiations but finally everything seemed to be as required. Even so, our colleague was still nervous about the arrangements when he arrived in Delhi, and his anxiety appeared to be well placed when the first of the agent's promised arrangements, someone to pick him and his wife up from Delhi airport, did not materialise.

Arrival in a foreign country is always a time of quiet anxiety. Will there be someone who understands me? Will I find a taxi? Will I actually find the hotel? Some airport arrival halls are more disquieting than others, and Delhi is one of the more disquieting, simply because of the crush of people arriving, waiting and *hustling*!

Fortunately our colleague had been to Delhi before and knew where the pre-paid taxi booth was and where the taxis waited. As long as the cab driver knew the hotel, everything should be okay. And it was. Our colleague and his wife duly arrived at the hotel, checked in and fell asleep.

The next day they were due to meet a representative of the agent. Naturally they were a little angry about the agent's failure to deliver at the airport, and a little apprehensive now about the rest of their arrangements, especially as they had already paid half of the costs up front and were due to settle the balance on meeting the representative. But even before the representative arrived they received a phone call. It was the agent wanting to know if everything was okay, with the hotel, with arrangements to date, and so on. When informed that the representative had failed to show up at the airport the agent sounded contrite, promising to find out what had gone wrong.

Later in the day our sceptical (and still angry) colleague met with the agent's representative and was handed, along with his tickets and hotel vouchers, an envelope. Inside the envelope were a mobile phone and a note. The note began with an apology, advising that the representative had been waiting at Delhi airport, but being inexperienced, had made the mistake of waiting in the wrong place. Our colleague could have responded by questioning why the person sent didn't even know the layout of the airport, but bit his tongue. The note, signed by the agent, explained the purpose of the mobile phone:

This mobile phone has a prepaid SIM card, which is yours to use during your stay in India. I have already entered my mobile phone number. Should anything go wrong, or you have reason to be unhappy about any of our arrangements please don't hesitate to contact me regardless of the time, day or night.

The mobile phone was an older Nokia model, and arrangements had already been made to return it via the hotel at the end of their holiday. The value of the SIM card was 300 Rupees, at the time, less than A$10.

The emotional impact this had on our colleague was immeasurable and can't be estimated in dollar terms.

During their three weeks in India our colleague and his wife received three phone calls from the agent, checking that they were enjoying themselves and confirming certain arrangements. They also called the agent three times, not to complain, but to rearrange a tour, or seek assistance with a late checkout. Before leaving India the agent made one final call asking for feedback and it was given honestly and in detail. Our colleague also reassured the agent that he would certainly be recommending his services to any friend or colleague looking for a travel agent in India.

You all have examples of the same type of thing happening in your lives. Everyone can recall an emotional moment that changed the relationship between you and a product, or a service. It could be that emotional high when you take delivery of your new car, or the contrasting emotional low when the car has broken down and the service manager informs you that the required part is unavailable, and sorry, no, we don't have a loan car available for the next three days.

The emotional impact of these kinds of experiences is far greater than the tangible. The benefit can't be described in features or even attributes, and the damage of the negative is almost impossible to gauge, as is the joy of the positive. Unfortunately we also know that the negative always outlives the positive.

So, if we're going to take advantage of this kind of emotion, if we are going to understand it, we need to become much more comfortable with the subjective. And that means we have to find a way to define the customer's experience, including the emotional aspects of the experience.

15
Moments of truth

We have used several stories from the airline industry throughout the book to support our case, or to prove a point about brands. No amount of money could have bought Qantas the brand recognition for its safety record that Dustin Hoffman's character in the film *Rainman* delivered. Safety was a critical issue in the 1990s, but today, Qantas, like Singapore Airlines, Emirates and Qatar, competes on the basis of superior service. Other airlines, such as Tiger Airways, compete on price. In fact, like Ryanair in Europe, Tiger Airways is developing a reputation for poor service, and a high level of customer complaints.

From the time air travel became affordable, service has been one of the key differentiators. Yet, in the late 70s and early 80s, the world's leading airlines were reporting a staggering combined loss of US$2 billion. At that time it must have been extremely inviting to look closely at trimming costs. One airline, Scandinavian Airlines System, went in the opposite direction under the guidance of a new Chief Executive Officer, Jan Carlzon, who was appointed in 1981 when the company had just reported a loss of US$30 million. Within 12 months, Carlzon had returned SAS to profitability and two years later the airline was named *Air Transport World's* "Airline of the Year".

In 1987 Carlzon published his account of the turnaround in his book *Moments of Truth*, which became a customer service bible, well-thumbed by CEOs and HR managers the world over. In truth it should have been required reading for every student studying branding and marketing.

Moments of Truth came from Carlzon's recognition that no organisation lives in the minds of its customers in the same way that it does in the minds of its executives. The sad truth for people in management is that their product or service only exists for a customer when the customer wants that product or service or comes into contact with the organisation that provides it. When that happens, as Carlzon astutely wrote in his book, there is a moment of truth that establishes whether that contact with your organisation, product or service is a positive experience, or a negative one.

Pick up the phone and ring your mobile phone service provider. What do you get? A real person, or a machine asking you to identify, in a few words, your reason for calling? And how do you feel about the machine — warm and responsive, or angry and abusive? Call your bank to see how long it takes to get you through the voice prompts to the service you need. Anything short of three minutes would be an all-time record. And as you wait to be attended to, reflect on how you feel about your bank.

How do you feel when you go into a retail store, let's say to buy some perfume or aftershave for your partner, and the sales attendant bends over backwards to make you feel comfortable and relaxed? Not only do you feel good about the sales attendant, you feel positive towards the store. Positive enough to make you want to come back?

The multiplying factor from a brand perspective makes these types of situations more and more complex, as we discovered when contemplating which brand gave most power to the *Mission Impossible* movie franchise — the production company, the star actor or the franchise itself.

Even the smallest change can have a significant impact. Most supermarkets use part-time employees to stock their shelves when they are either closed, or if they remain open 24 hours, when there are fewer people in the store. That means when you visit a supermarket late in the day there is a very good chance that some of the items on your shopping list won't be available. How do you react? Pick up an alternative brand? Or go home without it?

This common supermarket scenario has a varied impact on three brands. Firstly, the supermarket has just gone down in your estimation because it failed to have the brand you wanted, when you wanted it. Secondly, you're annoyed because the brand you prefer using isn't there, and by association, some of your annoyance rubs off on the supermarket as well. And thirdly, the replacement brand gets a boost because it was available and proves satisfactory.

It's like a giant game of dominoes, and as each one falls, a moment of truth occurs.

The principle Carlzon espoused in *Moments of Truth* was extraordinarily simple. In fact, so simple that he was able to define it in one short paragraph in his opening chapter:

Last year, each of our 10 million customers came in contact with approximately 5 SAS employees and this contact lasted an average of 15 seconds each time. Thus SAS is created 50 million times a year, 15 seconds at a time. These 50 million "moments of truth" are the moments that ultimately determine whether SAS will succeed or fail as a company. They are the moments when we must prove to our customers that SAS is their best alternative.[27]

Once you start thinking in terms of "moments of truth" you begin to see things from the perspective of your customers. And at that very moment you start to capture the real power of your brand.

The solution that Carlzon employed at SAS was to empower every employee at SAS with the authority to resolve individual moments of truth. In the opening story to his book he relates one such occurrence in which an American businessman travelling in Scandinavia had left his return airline ticket to Copenhagen on the sideboard in his Stockholm hotel. In the 80s, no-one travelled on electronic tickets, so the businessman was distraught to discover on his arrival at Stockholm airport that he did not have that all-important slip of paper. Imagine his surprise and pleasure when he confessed his forgetfulness to the SAS check-in attendant, who, instead of admonishing him and refusing to allow him to board, provided him with a boarding pass and then proceeded to call the businessman's hotel, verified through a bellhop that the ticket was indeed on the sideboard in his room and arranged for it to be couriered by taxi to the airport. Although the businessman made his flight, the story does not record how many more times he flew with SAS. We can only assume he became one of the company's best frequent flyers.

By defining each moment of truth from your customer's perspective you begin to understand how to orient your business to the customer's needs, as opposed to what you perceive those needs to be. That then becomes a measure to define the relationship between your brand and your customer. This is what brand strategists and brand managers do very well. They think like their customers because failure to do so will most likely see them out of a job.

You might argue that Carlzon's solution for SAS is not necessarily the appropriate solution for every circumstance. On the surface, that may appear to be the reality but if you dig deep enough you will see that there is an application for moments of truth in almost every instance, even when the brand appears to have no control over the situation.

Our poorly stocked supermarket shelf is a case in point. Each of the three brands involved — the supermarket, the brand that was out of stock and the brand replacement — were all part of the domino effect and each had a moment of truth. It would appear that only the supermarket is in control of its particular moment of truth. To maximise the moment, it could authorise someone to find the missing product for the customer — in fact, it could promote the service as a benefit.

The brand that was unavailable would appear to have no control over the moment of truth. However, the reverse is true because it also has the opportunity to turn a negative into a positive by carefully managing a campaign to offer a benefit or bonus should the customer ever find the shelves empty. Alternatively, the manufacturer has the power to withdraw supply from the supermarket chain if it is constantly disadvantaged by poor shelf management. Of course, the moment of truth for the replacement brand is when the customer trials the product and either finds it as good as the normal brand, better, or not as efficient.

We need to break down the premise of "moments of truth" into a manageable, practical process.

Carlzon had a particular problem exacerbated by the number of employees working for SAS and the extremely long lines of communication. Most companies simply don't have the same need.

In most developed and developing countries there is a very large percentage of small- and medium-sized enterprises. In Australia, small companies are classified as having less than 20 employees; medium companies have between 20 and 99 employees. These types of companies account for approximately 70 per cent of the Australian workforce. Carlzon had over 20,000 employees reporting through a complex structure of middle management, which he sought to simplify. That is what he needed to do to rescue the brand of SAS and that is what he did.

The issue isn't just size or communication. We need to establish a process that will enable you to identify the critical needs from a customer's perspective and the solutions you would put in place to deal with that person's needs.

Once again we can find some of the answers in the solutions proposed by quality management gurus such as Karl Albrecht.

Albrecht devised a simple tool to identify a customer's service experience. He called it the cycle of service. The same principle can be applied to your brand, so that when you review the brand experience from the customer's perspective, or each of the "moments of truth", we start to see some amazing perceptual opportunities arise. Let's call this tool our *brandcycle*.

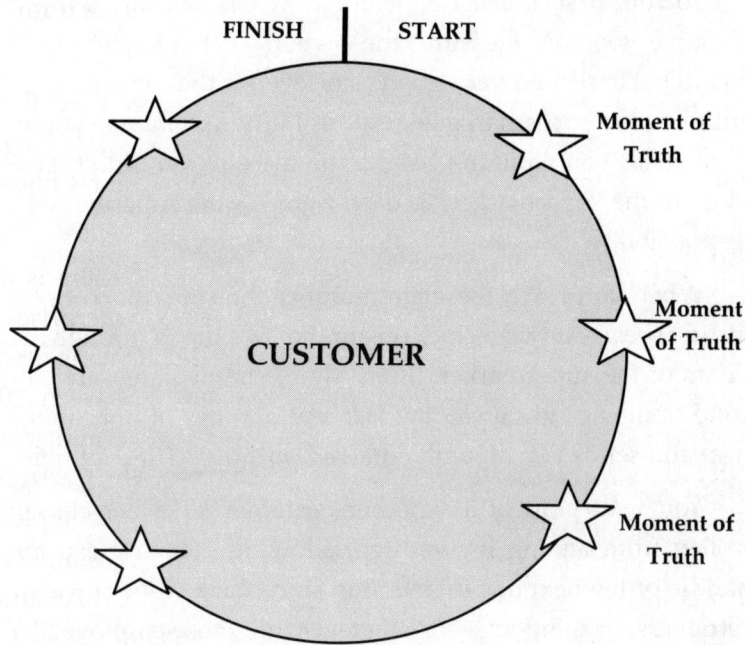

Imagine the face of a clock on which each of the 12 points represents an opportunity to interact with the company or organisation you want to do business with. Let's take it one step further. Imagine the clock face represents your last visit to a supermarket, and that your experience begins at the one o'clock position on the dial.

We all know the first part of that trip to the supermarket: the dreaded car park! You drive in and every space close to the entrance is full. Then you spot a park 50 metres away. Just as you spin the wheel to head in that direction another car comes from nowhere and pokes its nose into the space before you're even half way there. After five minutes of driving around in frustrating circles you find a park at the furthest point from the supermarket entrance. To make matters worse, it's a stinking hot day and you have to cross 70 metres of burning bitumen.

So your first contact on the brandcycle is, not surprisingly, negative. On this measure, the owners of the supermarket haven't started in a very good way, even if the car park isn't entirely the supermarket's responsibility. As far as you're concerned, you wouldn't have to be there if you didn't have to go to the supermarket, so darn right it's the supermarket's responsibility.

When you reach the main entrance the supermarket gets its first break. At two o'clock on our dial, we slip in through the doors of the supermarket. Bliss! Almost immediately the air-conditioning blows away the last few minutes of unbearable heat and sends you off with renewed purpose to find a trolley.

You wait politely as another customer jerks her chosen trolley from among its brethren, allowing you to grasp the handle of the next one in line. But, since the advent of trolley retrievers, or minders — or whatever title those employed by supermarkets to bring the trolleys back in from the weather are given — retrieving a trolley is not as simple as it used to be. Now it's an excursion on its own, with much huffing and puffing to shake it free. In the paroxysm of swearing and cursing, you don't notice that you have the only trolley in the whole supermarket with one square wheel.

So far, the score on our brandcycle, the score that tells us whether this is a positive or a negative experience, is one for and two against.

As our visit to the supermarket progresses, so does our experience. Take a ticket at the deli. Everyone serving is already occupied with another customer and you are number 84, with the overhead display showing the next in line is 71. Finally, after waiting for what seems like ages you are served and you move on, trying very hard not to blame the young deli assistant for your rapidly declining brand experience.

If you think things are going to improve, think again. Here you go, clunking down the first aisle behind your lop-sided trolley, armed with your trusty shopping list, and what do you find? The supermarket decided that this was the week it needed to rearrange the aisles. Or maybe the problem isn't that severe, perhaps it's three o'clock in the afternoon and the specials are all gone and the shelves are decidedly bare.

Finally, the torture is over. And if you're keeping count, by the end of the shopping visit you may be lucky to break even, with as many positive experiences as there are negatives.

What if we ran the same brandcycle on a bank?

Peter Drucker's maxim that the only purpose of a business is to create a customer comes immediately to mind.

In truth, does any bank see its role as creating customers, or is it merely offering a service that satisfies the demands of the shareholders for greater profits? Are banks really concerned about their brand, or just the company's financial performance in the marketplace?

We wonder how the banks fare in fulfilling Drucker's principle of creating customers. And is Albrecht's cycle of service the same as what we refer to as brand values?

We believe they are virtually inseparable; and by applying the brandcycle to your own brand, you will begin to understand what the customer experience could be like.

16
Asking the right questions

Putting the brandcycle to one side, nothing gets to the heart of the matter quicker than asking your customers what they think.

Boost Juice is one of Australia's recent brand success stories. The company commenced at the start of the new millennium with one store in Adelaide selling exotic but healthy juice drinks. Today the company has 219 outlets around the world, and the owner credits much of that success to asking what Boost Juice customers think.

In an interview with *The Australian* the owner of Boost Juice, Janine Allis, candidly said:

No one will tell you the truth like a customer. You don't get a filtered view from your customer — you get the warts and all — and I think that is what you are looking for because sometimes people tell you what you want to hear, not what is absolutely 100 per cent accurate.

The process of asking is another matter.

Satisfaction surveys have been a favourite method of many organisations to collect data about themselves and their performance. The problem with most satisfaction surveys is that they measure what the company thinks they should measure, rather than measuring what is important to the customer. We don't see the motivation behind satisfaction surveys as wrong necessarily, although we have seen politicians use inflated satisfaction figures to their advantage. Many people naively believe that these surveys are the panacea to their need for information about their customers. In many cases, the organisation would be better off giving the money to its favourite charity. More to the point, we do not believe that any organisation should be satisfied with a one-dimensional scorecard when they have the opportunity to use those same surveys to collect real, tangible information to help them understand and manage change.

Not that long ago, a research colleague was contracted by a statutory government body to undertake its satisfaction surveys. This was a massive undertaking involving several thousand staff, many thousands of customers and a large database of businesses. Without hesitation, and without concern that he was compounding the logistics, our colleague put forward the recommendation that instead of conducting a satisfaction survey, a fulfilment study be initiated in its place.

The difference is quite straightforward, but telling. A satisfaction survey measures the single dimension of satisfaction. On a scale of one to five, are you unsatisfied, somewhat satisfied, reasonably satisfied or very satisfied? This measure is applied to a series of statements requested by the client about the service, facilities and so on. On the other hand, a fulfilment survey measures the dimension of satisfaction as well as measuring the much more important degree of satisfaction relative to what the respondent thinks is important.

A fulfilment survey enables an organisation to prioritise how to direct its energy and resources to resolving customer needs; a satisfaction survey cannot. A fulfilment survey can never take the place of qualitative research that has been designed to unearth the customers' needs, or examine the detail of those needs, but it can save an organisation from wasting an enormous amount of money on things that don't need to be fixed.

Unfortunately, the life of the fulfilment survey our colleague recommended was short-lived. We won't bore you with complicated mathematical formula but suffice to say that the numerical results of a fulfilment survey cannot give you the level of inflated satisfaction that is all too often the egocentric outcome of satisfaction surveys. In this particular example, the client was unable to pat itself on the back and publish figures in the media with a headline that screams: *95 per cent satisfaction proves we were right!* So they sacked our colleague and reverted to satisfaction studies. Today that government body is no closer to understanding its customers' needs.

There are four steps to using the power of fulfilment in building your brand, each one designed to help you discover customer value.

- PART ONE identifies what *attributes* of the relationship are valued by the customer.
- PART TWO *prioritises* each attribute.
- PART THREE *compares* the performance of these attributes against the competition.
- PART FOUR asks how we can use this knowledge to establish our *point of difference*.

Easier said than done, we hear you say.

In fact, it is easier than you might think. In a previous chapter we asked whether you have ever attended a research focus group. Let's take it one step further: have you ever organised and facilitated a focus group?

Focus groups, and other forms of customer research, are not as intimidating as they may appear on the surface. We run focus groups all the time on behalf of organisations who want to get inside the heads of their customers. Like many things, confidence comes from the experience, and experience is an intriguing beast that comes in many forms. And focus groups work. Janine Allis, owner of Boost Juice, conducts regular focus groups to gain feedback from customers after they have visited one of the stores. In the same interview with *The Australian* we quoted from earlier, Janine Allis said what many modern managers already know: *"the day you stop listening to your customers and believing what everyone else says, you are in trouble"*.[29]

A focus group will usually comprise no more than ten people of similar interests, similar demographics, and depending on the subject matter, a mix of both sexes. They are conducted anywhere you can find a table with sufficient chairs around it for people to be able to sit comfortably, with the moderator or facilitator positioned in such a way that he or she can interact with every member of the group. This should mean that every group member can also see and interact with all the other participants. Ideally the room would be equipped with some form of recording device — audio, video, or both — and may feature a one-way mirror to enable clients to sit in another room and observe proceedings. A speaker system will allow clients to hear, as well as see what is said, but their room is soundproofed so that the research group can't hear any conversation that may occur between the clients.

The first thing people do when they enter a new environment is to check out their surroundings. People attending a focus group for the first time are exactly the same. They enter the room slowly, cautiously, usually as a group, rather than individually. There will be perhaps a slow look around the room and a reassuring welcome from the facilitator who may make a point of shaking each person's hand. Everyone is seated and asked to introduce themselves. As the introductions flow around the table people will be looking over their shoulder. Some may be intimidated by the sight of a mirror filling one wall of the room; others will observe the people around them; while others will reach out and fill a glass with juice or water, or perhaps help themselves to the food and refreshments that have been provided. Fairly normal, predictable actions and goings on. The participants are not so much nervous as uncertain: What questions are they going to be asked? Will they have the right answer, or will they look foolish in the eyes of the other people in the room?

Of course, that's the beauty of the beast. There are no right or wrong answers. What we need from the group members are their views and answers on the topic we are there to discuss.

The facilitator is very professional and understands the initial uncertainty and will allay any misgivings by explaining what is going to happen. He or she will also explain the purpose of the mirror, that there are probably clients behind the mirror, very eager to hear what the participants have to say, explain that the session will be recorded, and will probably finish the introduction by urging those who haven't yet done so to help themselves to refreshments. All of this is designed to achieve a level of comfort for the participants, to get them in the mood as quickly as possible given that, at best, we can expect to hold their attention for somewhere between 60 and 90 minutes. Of course it is our right to have their attention because these people are being paid to be there. Current rates vary but the average payment to attend could be as high as three or four times the average hourly income designated under the minimum wage.

So, all is in readiness for the group to begin. The facilitator will start by explaining the subject up for discussion. *Today we want to talk to you about... We want to find out what you think about...*

The facilitator will reiterate the point that there are no right or wrong answers, just opinions and perceptions and then ask a specific question to get everyone started.

On the table in front of the facilitator will be a topic guide. The topic guide is a series of questions or issues presented in a structured list to ensure that the facilitator covers the ground required. The topic guide ensures that each subsequent focus group, on the same subject, will be consistent in content, even if the answers are different.

1. **Introduction**   **10 minutes**
    i. Explain purpose of the research: to discuss Personal Training (PT) business management options
    ii. Explain the group process: no right or wrong answers, all responses are confidential and will be reported in aggregate
    iii. Explain audio and video taping for reporting purposes only
    iv. Duration of approximately 1.5 hours
    v. Participants introduce themselves:
        a. Tell me a bit about yourself, why you chose to become a personal trainer

    b. What are your plans for the future?

2. **The good and bad things about the PT business   20 minutes**

    i. What do you enjoy most about the business? Explore why.

    ii. What do you enjoy least? Explore further. Is the group consistent? Probe for issues regarding client management, files, record keeping, income /cash flow.

    iii. How do you currently manage these functions? What is good/bad about the process you use? If manual, probe for time issues; if using another system, explore its obvious strengths and weaknesses.

3. **Exploring the possibilities   20 minutes**

    i. What is the single thing you would do to improve your current system? Why? What would be the benefit of that particular change? Explore from the group's perspective. Do they all agree? Are there common issues? Explore specifics if not covered, from both a business management perspective and a client perspective, for example:

        a. Track and manage your PT sessions (business and client)

        b. Record keeping (business)

        c. Income and cash flow

        d. Payment records

    ii. Is tracking and managing the progress and results of each client important to your business? Explore how they currently manage this. Efficient, cost effective, time effective?

   iii. How important is it to you that you can access your bookings and client records quickly, where and when you need to?

4. **Product Demonstration**   20 minutes

   i. Introduce the product, brief background. Allow as much time as possible for participants to use the product.

5. **Consumer Benefits**   20 minutes

   i. How do you rate the product as a PT management tool? Would it meet some or all of your needs? None of your needs?

   ii. Which feature would you rate highest? Which feature would you use most frequently? Which feature wouldn't you use?

   iii. How would this product benefit your business? If not offered, probe for more time to focus on clients, assistance with cash flow.

   iv. What single feature would you add to the product?

   v. How much do you believe such a system would cost per month? What would you be prepared to pay?

      a. In summing up what we have talked about today, how do you feel about the overall value of this product?

This topic guide was used to explore the financial management needs of personal trainers. They are a key part of the burgeoning global fitness industry given the current problems of obesity and unhealthy eating and living habits, and usually are small and medium enterprises.

What is important to understand about the topic guide is that it leads into the subject, rather than opening directly on what we may want to know. The facilitator is actually setting the scene, like any good novelist will do when writing a story, or artist when painting a picture. The scene is the environment in which the product or service has to operate. So we explore the problems and issues that have the potential to affect the product before we actually move onto specifics about the product and the needs of the participants relative to the product. Everything about the structure is designed to keep the discussion as neutral as possible, without leading the participants or imposing any preconceived ideas or preferences the owners of the product or service may have.

The product under discussion in the focus group is designed to help personal trainers to more effectively and efficiently manage their clients and their business. This discussion, like all others, is designed to tease out what the group members see as the most critical aspects of their business that need improvement, prior to any discussion on how they would make those improvements occur.

The best way to learn is to participate. If you've never been invited to a focus group, check around for a local research company, find out who does their recruiting and get your name and demographic details on their database. We promise you, it won't be long before you're invited along to a focus group dealing with something that you are considered to be a prime target for. Then, participate, but also take the time to observe how the facilitator manages the session and the way the questions are structured to avoid leading participants to a preferred conclusion. Get a feel for the type of questions that prompt people to open up, rather than respond with a yes or no.

What the focus group is forcing you to do is act like the consumer you are and consider the product from a consumer's perspective. Learn that lesson well, apply the principle to your own business and you have taken another step along the path to understanding the power of brands.

Of course, the focus group is only one of a range of techniques that you can use to gather information. If you're in the training business, next time you're holding a session with a group of people, set aside 30 minutes to ask them some questions. Or invite a group of employees in for a cup of coffee and ask them to role play the part of customers. Stop people in the street and ask them what they think about an aspect of their life that involves your product or service and what they would do to improve it. Once you've set the scene you can introduce your specific product, its features and ask about what they think. Shy about stopping people in the street? Well, use the same technique with friends and family. The secret is to ask the right questions so that people don't give you the answer they think you want to hear, and that requires some practice. But use family members as guinea pigs. From our experience, once you get over the reluctance and shyness to approach people, the process becomes almost addictive. You want to ask people questions.

That's how you get the information, but let's revisit what we are seeking to find out by wearing the customer or consumer's hat.

We have already defined the four parts of fulfilment: one, identifying what attributes of the relationship the customer values; two, prioritising each attribute, relative to the others; three, comparing the performance of these attributes against the competition; and, four, asking how we can use this knowledge to establish our point of difference.

The next step is to identify the questions or topics we need to ask to get to the core of this.

To identify what attributes customers value, we need to ask questions that will examine the place in which they use the product or service and how they use it. What does it do for them? What other products or services does it provide a substitute for? Why do they need the product or service in the first place? We need to understand how important the product or service is to them in a generic sense before we look at whether our product or service fulfils their need better than another.

If the topic was training, our starting point might be asking them to think about what opportunities are available to the customer to undertake training; what they understand are the benefits of each of the different options; and what they believe would be the advantage to them of undertaking that particular form of training in the first place. Does it advantage them, or their employer? Do they want it to advantage them, or their employer? Much of getting to the emotional connection occurs before we examine what the benefits of our product are.

What if we were asked to research a new motor vehicle insurance company to understand the attributes and benefits from a consumer's perspective. Where would you start?

Again, the answer is not in the specifics of the product being offered, but in the environment in which the product needs to exist. However, anyone in the insurance business will already have a depth of knowledge about motivations and needs in their field. Like Revlon's observation linking lipstick to "hope", people purchase insurance for one reason only: "peace of mind". It is the necessary evil we must have, regardless of whether the insurance is on your life, your home or your car. The one underpinning truth is that you don't ever want to use it.

So how much do we need to dig into this part of people's lives in a focus group to understand the attributes and benefits of the new car insurance product? The answer may surprise you.

We would spend a significant amount of time exploring this part of the insurance psyche because here is a likely place to discover the emotional connection to link your brand to your customer. Even though it may be a generic proposition, making the participants in a focus group explore the reasons that they buy insurance gives you the opportunity to understand their frustrations. Expressions that we have already used, such as "necessary evil" will abound, but dig a little further and you may well come up with an insight that leads to a powerful brand promise.

Insurance group NRMA launched its latest advertising blitz with the theme *"Unworry"*. The word doesn't even exist in the English language, so what did they mean?

In fact, NRMA was cleverly reflecting on the customer's need to achieve peace of mind. There were no images of horrific car crashes, or people being rushed to hospital or the mortuary. Instead, the NRMA campaign shows a positive, optimistic take on life that encourages people not to worry about life's "what ifs". Unworry is the word they use to persuade people to *stop* worrying. "Unworry" connects the customer to the brand at an emotional level.

17
Finding the right answers

Do you know what the total quality management (TQM) gurus call this part of the solution? They use descriptions such as "customer values" or even "customer value *package*". Karl Albrecht exalted his followers to be *"something special to someone in particular."* On the other hand, marketing gurus such as Phillip Kotler encourage you to identify market opportunities and *develop targeted value offerings*.

The two ideas and the two supposedly different principles are surprisingly similar. The marketing principle Kotler espouses is that wherever there is a need, there is a market, and that the smart entrepreneur simply needs to find the best way to deliver the solution to that need. TQM exponents, such as Albrecht, argue that their TQM proposition is the secret to creating a sustainable competitive advantage. The marketing gurus describe this as their USP: the *unique selling proposition* that makes what you are selling irresistible to the buyer.

We concur!

Great brand strategists see opportunities everywhere and apply the same customer-centric thinking that is the essence of great marketing and the cornerstone of powerful quality management. Why should it be surprising that the two things are so compatible?

And the smartest way to achieve the best results is relatively simple and straightforward: all you need to do is think, and respond, like a consumer.

We have said repeatedly that thinking like a customer is the most critical attribute you need to build powerful brands, followed closely by the capacity to understand the emotional imperative that is intrinsically linked to those thought processes. But that means you not only need to learn how to ask the questions, but also the right questions to ask.

The good news is that when it comes to asking the right questions to ensure you get the right answers, the rules and frameworks are simple and straightforward.

For starters there are only three situations that drive the market opportunities underpinning brands. Not a dozen, not 10, not five, just three. So the framework you are going to be operating in can be defined quickly and painlessly.

The first market opportunity is *supplying something in short supply*.

If something is in short supply, people will queue to buy it and little energy is required to make money. Many people who have been able to corner a monopoly have become obscenely wealthy as a result, without having to worry too much about Kotler's principles, Albrecht's systems or brand DNA.

At the opposite end of the spectrum is *supplying a completely new product or service*. In this case, the market opportunity is more about the consumer's capacity to visualise and find value in what you're offering, than differentiating value between similar products. Most of us could not imagine the iPhone before Apple invented it. To suggest the idea of a video recorder 40 years ago would have had people laughing at you. Today, Blu-ray technology is already outdated.

There are, of course, an enormous number of people who have incredible talent to innovate and create, and they will probably never need to look beyond this second market opportunity.

The third opportunity is *supplying an existing product or service, in a new or better way.*

Most market opportunities sit in this group. This is also where brands have to do their hardest work.

To supply something in a new way, or in a better way, obviously requires you to be different. And the simplest way to determine how you can be different is to ask people who use the product or service what they want. And the question you want to start with is whether they have any problems with their current brand.

Their response, although predictable, will be incredibly informative:

"My computer is too slow."

"My mobile phone provider charges like a wounded bull."

"The tyres on my car don't last 30,000 kilometres."

After they have bombarded you with the list of problems or deficiencies, ask them what their wish list would be. Asking for a wish list is not the same as asking them to imagine something beyond their scope. Effectively, you are asking: What if? And, of course, this is inextricably linked to the "What's in it for me?" question.

"I wish I could pay my insurance monthly."

"I would give anything to stop people ringing at night to sell me something."

"Wouldn't it be great if you had a phone that worked by touching the screen?"

"True bliss would be having politicians you could trust."

What a mixed bag of problems and opportunities.

Computers have advanced in leaps and bounds since the first PCs were introduced in the late 70s and early 80s. Start-up times then weren't the problem — there was very little program grunt that needed to be started. Start-up became an opportunity as computers were made more compact, faster, with greater capacity; or, in other words, as the market became more sophisticated. What had seemed like science fiction became the everyday, and our needs and demands changed irrevocably.

Competition in the mobile phone sector has resulted in charges in most countries falling dramatically, (except where there are monopolies over the network, such as in Australia). In a monopoly much of the focus on mobile phone marketing is about "value adding", or trying to demonstrate that the price tag is justified.

Similarly, although car manufacturers may not always take heed, astute tyre manufacturers do. To replace a set of tyres costs serious money, so the warranty periods, or promises of tyre life are getting longer and longer. Don't be surprised if one day you see a claim offering a guarantee on the tyres for as long as you keep the car.

Most insurance companies now provide customers with a monthly payment scheme that doesn't penalise them too hard; a service to block your phone number from pests has been created; and Apple, we suspect, were ahead of the customer who suggested a touch phone. As for the politicians, unfortunately we don't know if the Apple computer gurus could resolve that.

It is standard fare for most market research companies to examine products in this manner. Their simplest methodology is to interview a group of consumers and ask them to design the ideal product or service in the category. They will then report back to the client with a list of features that could provide the benefits the consumers are seeking.

You may finish up with some wonderfully wild and expensive ideas, but you will also come up with some gems. Unfortunately, almost every methodology employed to unearth customer needs requires you to ask questions. So, if you are the shy, retiring type we would suggest you employ someone else to undertake the task.

The *consumption chain* method is another employed by market researchers to seek out opportunities. In simple terms this is the principle that probably provided Albrecht with the premise behind his cycle of service.

The supply chain principle is simple enough: different components play their role in getting the raw material into the hands of the consumer. The consumption chain, which is akin to the cycle of service, provides researchers with a process to analyse each step the consumers take in acquiring, using and then disposing of the product. What they are looking for at each step is an opportunity, or a better way to do it from the consumer's perspective.

An article by MacMillan and McGrath in the *Harvard Business Review* provided a succinct list of the questions we need to ask.

1. How do people become aware of their need for your product or service?
2. How do consumers find your offering?
3. How do consumers make their final selection?
4. How do consumers order and purchase your product or offering?
5. How is your product or service delivered?
6. What happens when your product or service is delivered?
7. How is your product installed?
8. How is your product or service paid for?
9. How is your product stored?
10. How is your product moved around?
11. What is the customer really using your product for?
12. What do customers need help with when they use your product?
13. What about returns or exchanges?
14. How is your product repaired or serviced?
15. What happens when your product is disposed of or no longer used?

The direct debit industry has grown exponentially in a business environment that has seen many services outsourced, including the collection of money. A company set up to process direct debits will see opportunities to expand its business through a broad range of different retail outlets, and service and utility providers. No doubt you have either used, or are currently using, one of these providers to make monthly payments on your car, your telephone bill, your gas bill and so on. What the direct debit company appreciates is that every organisation that uses its services may have the same ultimate problem: the collection of money. But the reason each company uses the service is potentially different, and the customers that they are pitching the service to have different motivations. An electrical retailer may require a direct debit facility to sell goods online while a gymnasium will use the same facility to collect members' monthly fees.

In the previous chapter we explored the technique of creating a topic guide to determine a consumer's response to WIFM. The example shown was providing the direct debit facility to personal trainers.

As a group of people, personal trainers will have much in common with each other, and therefore their motivations have strong constants. However, the WIFM perspective of an energy utility or a telco is significantly different, and unless the direct debit company understands this, and looks for these differentials, it will fail to provide the value that is possible. Granted, it will provide a service, and the service may be adequate, until it has some serious competition.

Our process borrows from market research principles but we have framed it with apologies to the Five P's of Marketing. Instead of *Product, Price, Promotion, Place and Perception,* (the original four p's of marketing have recently been extended to incorporate perceptions), we want to suggest the **Five P's of Brand Value**.

1. **PLACE:** The physical environment in which you experience the product or service. Place is particularly relevant to service delivery.

2. **PROPERTIES:** Our awareness, understanding or sense of a product or service; impressions created through touch, taste, smell and visual triggers.
3. **PEOPLE:** The experience we have with the 'people' component of service and support; the levels of friendliness, courtesy and efficiency.
4. **PROCESS:** This is wide ranging and takes into account any part of the process that is a physical part of the experience including: waiting in a queue; providing information (including the information that is contained on a sign or other point of sale explaining part of the process); the package that the product comes in; and the terms of a contract.
5. **PRICE:** This is not just the price but the way the price is determined, managed or even represented to the customer.

So, how do we apply the five p's of brand value to a product or service? What are we looking for?

A colleague of ours runs a business printing balloons — let's call it *Better Balloons,* located in an industrial shed on an estate only 15 kilometers from the city's GPO. He bought the business several years ago at a time when its principal customer base was corporations that wanted large numbers of balloons printed with their logo or artwork for a particular promotional campaign. Fifty per cent of his customers came from his home state and included major retailers and the state lottery business; the remaining 50 per cent came from interstate. When he first purchased the business, most trading was transacted over the phone, but increasingly more is being done via the web and email. The product is delivered by fast courier.

Our colleague has expanded the business by developing the capacity to print on many surfaces: corflute for signs, canvas for banners, ceramics for coffee cups, vinyl for stickers and paper for a range of uses.

Now he has decided to go into the retail end, selling short runs of balloons to mums and dads as well as retaining the corporate market. This means he will need to rethink significant parts of his business to enable him to deal with one-off customers, servicing events such as parties and weddings. To complicate his life, it is unlikely that these new retail customers will be able to provide him with artwork, in the way his corporate customers do.

As a first step in marketing his new service he has secured a billboard on one of the major arterials into the city. He hopes it will be seen by mums, and other prospective targets looking for balloons to make their parties more personal, and in some cases, more professional.

Let's look at his business through the perspective of our "five p's", the first of which is **place**.

Our reading of the future for the Better Balloons brand is that place is irrelevant. Samples of his work and finished product can be sent by courier very quickly to anywhere in the world. He already conducts most of his business over the phone or via the web, and unless he intends to change this, place is not the issue. In many cases, the internet makes location largely irrelevant; however, were he located a significant distance from convenient transport hubs he would have to reappraise his position due to increasing delivery costs. Only by locating his business in a busy shopping precinct would he maximise the attribute of place and turn it into a benefit. But this would then become more a dilemma about dividing his focus between two completely different targets.

Secondly we need to look at his business from the perspective of **properties**: the touch, taste, smell, visual and perceptual triggers. The visual impact of the balloons is what attracts people to them in the first place. The corporate clients use them as promotional items to attract attention. Mums use them to appease the increasing expectations and demands of children's parties, or their own social events. Balloons are three-dimensional, but signs are usually two-dimensional, and the power of the message they portray is, in part, dependent upon the quality of the printed message and how bright or how clear it is when the balloon is fully inflated or the sign erected.

The feel and smell of the balloons is less important but may help to convey the impression of durability. The promise of durability and the customer's preparedness to accept that promise will obviously have a bearing on price and expectation. The most likely attribute of properties, which we will be able to turn into a powerful benefit, is print quality and flexibility.

The third of our "five p's" is **people**. Quality people, with the right skills are paramount in any business. In the printing business it is critical that the right people are in the key roles of pre-press and production. Without them, you cannot expect to go out and cultivate custom. Then you need the right skills to deal with your customers. Our colleague has employed a group of people for whom nothing ever seems to be too much trouble; they are unfailingly courteous, and deliver on time, if not ahead of time. People are a key attribute, but how important is this "p" to our customer, who may well finish up ordering online and never see anyone but the courier? And given that purchases may not amount to more than double-digit cost, will the quality of the backroom production team be of any import whatsoever?

The fourth "p" is **process**. We have no direct experience of the back end of our colleague's business. All we know is that things run smoothly from our perspective as a customer. One of the positive joys of dealing with Better Balloons is the sense of being its only customer, not because we are, but because the sense of not being rushed fosters this sentiment. And it's the same whether you are at the front counter or on the phone.

Finally, the fifth "p" of **price**. Once again, we must confront the dilemma of expansion. When our colleague's business was corporate, price was probably only one of a number of criteria in the purchaser's consideration. The subtle difference between being competitive rather than cheaper would have been a factor. On-time delivery and a certain expectation of quality would have been other factors encouraging the customer to choose Better Balloons. By heading down the retail path, with short runs of *Happy 7th Birthday Matthew*, price becomes a much more critical question.

Now all we need to determine from a customer's perspective is which of these benefits, or combination of benefits, is the key for the future of Better Balloons.

18

At the heart of business planning

In the foreword, we contended that every business can build a successful brand if the owners and managers of that business are prepared to put their brand at the centre of their thinking, at the very heart of their business strategy. We are not the first to propose a different or alternative view to strategic planning. Albrecht's view focused on quality; he argues that quality should not only be the strategic imperative of the whole organisation, but suggested that it should *subsume* the planning process.

Jan Carlzon's *Moments of Truth* was a landmark in service culture for managers in the 1980s. Many of the ideas propounded by Carlzon were picked up and expanded over the next decade by total quality management purveyors such as Albrecht, as testament to the perceived importance of a service ethic. This had the effect of consolidating the value of service as a critical strategic planning platform.

We believe that the demise of the service ethic was also inevitable, in large part because of the enormous lip-service paid to the principle that the customer is king, or queen. Many companies spruik this ethos from tall buildings and, with faint memories of Carlzon trying to escape from the dark corners of their minds, present customer service as their most important value. But do they really deliver, and can they sustain it for the long haul?

In Australia many large banks have become notorious for poor customer service. The key reason behind the successful rise of smaller banks and other financial institutions has been their capacity to understand and implement a strong customer focus. The impact of these newcomers has been significant, forcing the recalcitrant majors to publicly declare their intentions to revert to good, old-fashioned service. One bank took the step of reinventing the role of bank managers, hiring several hundred such managers and reopening branches that had been closed. Another boldly declared, through an advertising campaign: ***Change your bank*** We are.

This promise came after a new CEO was appointed to the National Australia Bank, one of Australia's four major banks. He announced that the bank had, for too long, neglected its customers, and it was time for change. A survey conducted by Roy Morgan Research in May 2009 confirmed the bank had the worst satisfaction rating among personal and business customers of the four majors, with less than 55.6 per cent of customers satisfied with the bank's performance, compared with a high of 87.9 per cent of customers satisfied with their building society.

NAB's advertising promise not only intimated, but declared, that this needed to change:

At NAB, our aim is to do whatever it takes to improve the way you bank with us. We've listened to your feedback and are continuing to introduce more initiatives that will benefit each and every one of our customers.

Such a promise is a massive undertaking by any organisation. Jan Carlzon understood that to change the service culture of SAS would involve thousands of employees and would require each one of them to understand and implement the changes required, not simply pay lip-service to them. A bank such as NAB, with millions of customers around the country, must be absolutely confident that it can deliver on the promises it makes, or it will burn more prospective customers than it will gain. What is even more compelling is that advertising campaigns designed to attract new customers are there for the whole world to see, including existing customers whose expectations will undoubtedly rise and who will become even sterner critics if the promise is not fulfilled.

For 40 or 50 years, Qantas rivalled the best airlines in the world for the quality of its customer service. However, in the past decade, Qantas has paid dearly for the management team taking its eye off customer service. In his book, *The men who killed Qantas*, Matthew Benns contends that customer service, alongside safety, was sacrificed by the senior executives of Qantas to improve the bottom line. In 2009, Qantas also appointed a new CEO who announced that customer service and safety would return as his, and the airline's, number one priority. The CEO began his tenure by promising to find ways to reduce the number of late arrivals and long turnaround times.

But can these promises last in the face of financial imperatives that weigh heavily on the management of Qantas and NAB?

We suspect that the cycle will see Qantas services improve and NAB shake out the lethargy, for a while. But like so many other business 'fads', the concepts that Albrecht pushed under the premise of TQM have faded away before, to languish in the cupboards of HR managers around the world. These concepts only resurface temporarily when the media heat conspires with customer dissatisfaction.

Once again, the rally cry of *the customer is king* will climb to the top of the pile. Each time there is talk of a revolution, but it has never survived.

The concepts of marketing and brand live precarious existences, just as customer focus does. All too often marketing managers and brand managers are hidden down the same corridors as the HR managers, well away from the centre of power within the organisation. Yet, to all intents and purposes, the 'marketing buck' must stop with the Managing Director or CEO, and the marketing ethos must be all-pervasive. If we accept Drucker's observation that the only definition of business purpose is to create a customer, we have to accept that marketing is at the forefront of this endeavour.

Many business authors acknowledge that the marketing function is badly misrepresented and often misunderstood within organisations. These authors reject the simplistic view that marketing is selling. In fact, Drucker observed that the aim of marketing is to make selling superfluous; if the product or service is right and completely meets the needs of the consumer, there will be little point in building large sales teams because the product or service will sell itself.

We get confused whenever we see a business card announcing someone's position as *Sales & Marketing Manager*. Sales is a function of marketing and this particular job title is testament to the ignorance about marketing in the business world.

So, we are presented with a dilemma. Customer service marketing is not always well understood, nor is its importance within the organisation always accorded proper recognition. Yet marketing is the primary driver of brand building. And if our entire proposition outlined in this book is not to come crashing back to earth with a thud, or be buried alongside TQM's service principles, we need business people to rise above their preconceived notions or beliefs about the purpose or role of marketing and understand that the *values of service principles*, and the *values of brand* are inextricably linked with company performance.

If we intend to locate the brand at the centre, or heart, of a business, we need to understand the purpose and process of planning.

In our opinion too many strategic planners try, perhaps deliberately, to give the impression that planning is a complex process best left to the consultants. The truth is, as long as you understand the process, anyone can, and we strongly urge, should, prepare a strategic plan for his or her business.

We have discussed at length the principle that if you can't define a product, you can't sell it. Similarly if you can't define a business, what its purpose is, and where it is heading, how can you effectively maximise the return? However, we understand that when many of us hear words such as *vision* and *mission* associated with strategic planning, we tend to cringe and shy away from them. But in their simplest form these are potentially the most powerful foundations on which to build your brand.

Consider the classic exchange when Alice spoke to the cat, in Lewis Carroll's *Through the Looking Glass*:

Alice asked, *"Which way should I go?"*

The cat replied with the observation, *"That depends on where you are going"*.

Alice immediately cried, *"I don't know where I'm going!"*

To which the cat gave the only reply it could: *"Then it doesn't matter which way you go"*.

That's what strategic planning is about; it is simply a road map, with instructions on how to get where you're going. But first you must know the destination and how you plan to reach it.

19
I have a dream

Mention the words *strategic planning* and watch people's eyes glaze over. You can almost hear the cynicism ticking over in their heads when they contemplate their *vision* or *mission*. If those remarks resonate with your "cynicism", please, stay with us, because we hope we can give you a different, fresher and more credible perspective on the whole process.

When we talked about Levitt's concept of marketing myopia we reflected on his example of the US railways, and their inability to think outside the square relative to the business they were in. Defining what business you are in is a critical component of the strategic planning process. We will elaborate more on that shortly, but for the moment we want to examine how redefining your business can be incredibly motivating, not just for you as the owner or manager, but for your staff and your stakeholders, perhaps even your customers.

How exciting would it have been for the employees of the US railways to realise that they were a part of something much bigger than they thought? What opportunities would that have opened up for them? Not just business opportunities and wealth creation (which hopefully would have flowed onto them) but job and career opportunities. For employees who always dreamt of moving to another city, could such a change have opened up that opportunity? Instead of sideways promotions, which can be the bane of some organisations, could there have been opportunities to manage new operations or to take their experience into another part of the supply chain, without having to look for a new company to work for? (Don't forget that in the 1950s and 60s a job for life was the ambition of everyone, not a millstone around their necks.)

There is a classic case study about Avis, the car rental company that has been competing with Hertz for the number one position in that industry for decades. To our minds the Avis story brings together much of what we have been discussing about brands, beginning with the intriguing story about how Avis coined the phrase: *We Try Harder*.

In 1962 Robert C. Townsend was appointed president of Avis following a long period of sustained losses. As one of his early initiatives, Townsend determined that Avis needed to freshen up its image. He appointed Doyle Dane Bernbach, a young and extremely creative advertising agency, to help turn the business around. *We Try Harder* came out of the union, a phrase destined to be much more than just an advertising line or catchcry.

There is conjecture both within, and outside, the company, about whether the original campaign was based on the fact that Avis was number two in the market, and therefore *had to try harder* to gain customers or, because of the precarious nature of the company, it meant *we try harder because we have to*. Both stories have their antecedents. The *number two* theory is supported by the fact that a campaign using the phrase *Avis is only No. 2* had already been written, at a time when the company had sustained 13 years of continuous losses. The previous year had seen a revenue position of only US$ 34 million and a loss of US$ 3.2 million. One year later Avis' revenue had jumped to US$ 38 million with a profit of US$ 1.2 million.

The story and principle of 'trying harder because you are number two' has been included in just about every advertising book ever written. Yet, in our minds, the important lesson to be learnt from Avis occurred in conjunction with, and alongside, its clever advertising strategy, developed as Townsend and his senior management team sat down to review the company's strategic plan.

Virtually every strategic planning session follows a predictable formula, which has changed very little since Townsend and his executive sat down together. The four steps shown in the following chart provide the framework, and although the ways to describe the steps may vary, the outcomes are constant.

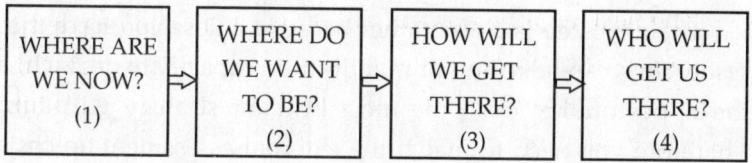

The first step in the process is an analysis of where your brand is at this particular point in time. You need to look both internally and externally, starting with an assessment from your perspective of the environment your brand exists within. It is hardly ever a constant environment. Customers change their habits, governments change their regulations and the economic climate is an ever-moving trial for even the strongest companies. This review is critical in understanding the circumstances that are most likely to impact on your potential success and why.

In a SWOT analysis (strengths, weaknesses, opportunities and threats), these circumstances would underline both your opportunities, and your threats. The review would logically include an assessment of the market; a close look at the impact of social and demographic factors on your business; consideration of how the economy could change and what the variable could mean; and an analysis of your competition, particularly the chance that they could match you, outflank you, or heaven forbid, already be better than you. The review would embrace the impact of technology and other production issues; possible changes the government could make to the regulatory environment in which you exist; and finally, and perhaps the most critical, an assessment of all the needs, beliefs and desires of your customers and potential customers.

The end result of this examination is a short list of opportunities and threats that must be managed effectively for you to succeed.

The next step is a no-brainer because unless you have the resourcing, capitalisation or mobilisation capacity to deal with the opportunities, even the most brilliant strategy will fail. Therefore you need to match the external assessment against an internal review of your strengths and weaknesses. If the opportunity is to expand, you need to review your own human resources and management strengths; if the opportunity is to introduce a new product, you will need the capacity and the financing to make sure you don't fall short.

Conversely, your business may be under threat from a rapidly improving competitor and you need to quickly resolve the training weaknesses in your system to be able to respond. Or, a change in the demographic profile of your potential customers means you have a weakness in your customer profiling tool and need to address the shift but don't have the resources to do so.

There is, more often than not, a blurring between these two assessments. Strengths and weaknesses begin to emerge when you are looking at the external factors. Equally, a review of your strengths and weaknesses may cause you to revisit some of the external issues with a more critical eye.

As you progress through these assessments you will become aware of factors that are largely beyond your control but which will have an impact on your final strategy. You will need to make assumptions about the likely impact and factor those assumptions into your planning, and be ready to change those assumptions if the market proves you wrong. Your assumptions might include the potential size of the market, which doesn't eventuate; the likely strength of your competitors, who go on to exceed your assumed estimate; or a demographic shift that is offset by a change in government migration planning.

This brings us to the intriguing culmination to the Avis story, involving the great Bill Bernbach's role. Bernbach was one of the founders of modern advertising, alongside other greats such as David Ogilvy and Leo Burnett. He is reputed to have been a man of strong principle and would have always spoken his mind, regardless of the client's ultimate response. If he believed that a promise couldn't be delivered he would say so. His contact with Avis pre-dates his appointment by Robert Townsend and the moment when his agency put pen to paper to flesh out the *"We Try Harder"* campaign. According to folklore, Bernbach had been approached by Avis to handle its advertising but had initially refused to do so. He is on record urging Avis to overhaul its customer service and upgrade its product. His uncompromising stance involved his belief that *"it is always a mistake to make good advertising for a bad product"*.

Shortly afterwards, Townsend persuaded Bernbach to reconsider his decision to turn down the US$2 million account. Bernbach finally agreed, and in the first meeting asked Townsend and the executives of Avis the simple WIFM question: *"Why does anybody ever rent a car from Avis?"* Their response, following the pain of years of losses and always trailing Hertz was, *"We try harder, because we have to"*. Of course, the rest is now advertising history but that, fortunately, is not where this story ends.

We will never know if the president of Avis had been motivated by Bernbach's urging to get its customer service on track, but in 1962 Robert Townsend called his executive together, we presume with the authority of the Avis board, and sat down for the first of many strategic planning sessions. When the group considered the critical questions, *where they are*, and *where they want to be*, perhaps Townsend recalled Ted Levitt's *Harvard Business Review* article questioning the short-sightedness of the US railways when they defined their business.

Without doubt Townsend would have looked at the members of the executive, some of whom had been there since Avis' inception, and asked them what business they believed Avis was in.

In the back of his mind Townsend suspected that the company had incorrectly defined itself as being in the car rental business. After Townsend considered the mission of Avis, he came up with an unexpected, and probably unwelcome, conclusion.

What is the most obvious waste or by-product of the car rental business? The answer is obvious, and if you correctly identified cars, you win the prize! Townsend's analysis showed him that Avis created enough waste products to effectively make the company the world's second largest producer of used cars, and that, Townsend concluded, was the business Avis was in.

The shift in business focus and strategies created by such a change is profound. At its very simplest level the change means that one day you are considering how to extract the maximum kilometre return from each rental vehicle; the next you are looking at ways to minimise the number of kilometres to increase the return value of each vehicle in the used market.

Think about the change in mindset that requires among managers and employees. Before the change they're looking for ways to minimise maintenance costs yet still get 50,000 rental kilometres out of each vehicle. After the change their focus is to achieve a level of maintenance quality that would put most private owners to shame. One minute they're considering bulk change-over deals with wholesalers, the next they're learning how to manage used car lots. With one simple decision you've opened up a range of career paths in your company that never existed before.

And the bottom line? Not only has the appearance, performance and age of your rental product changed dramatically for the better, your capacity to satisfy customers has jumped through the roof.

To us, Townsend's conclusion about the business Avis was in was far more defining than a clever advertising line, regardless of how brilliant that advertising slogan might be.

Yet the two things work hand in hand perfectly as we will see shortly.

We don't know the workings of Townsend's executive as the members contemplated their current position, or their desired position. We can make a reasonable assumption that they had conducted a thorough internal and external assessment of their company in order to arrive at the new definition of their business. When they reached the point of looking ahead, they had defined the business they were in but now they needed to turn that new understanding into an achievable way forward.

For the moment let's take a new, fresh look at strategic planning, the way Townsend did. Let's ignore the sceptics who will try to label strategic planning as restrictive and formulaic, and ignore those consultants who will attempt to present their process as the "definitive" one. The value of strategic planning is not in the process, and it definitely shouldn't be restrictive, or prescriptive. In fact, how can something that assists in defining your business be anything but liberating?

But that means we need to deal with the one word that makes so many people cringe: *vision*.

Some have called the *vision* a "dream with a date" because it identifies what and where the organisation wants to be at some time in the future. Other planners have used the term "envisioning" and quote Martin Luther King's famous *"I have a dream"* speech, which he delivered in Washington DC in 1963. What is consistent among strategic planners is their commitment to the central role of the *vision* in strategic planning.

What must be clearly understood is that an organisation's *vision* does not need to belong to the public. It is *your dream*, not that of others, even though it will obviously have a significant influence on your decision-making and how you allocate resources. Share it if you wish, but remember, you don't have to.

We suspect that people shy away from visioning because they are uncomfortable with both the word and the implications it has, not to mention the raised eyebrows in the pub later when your mates ask you what you did today. *"Well, we created a vision, actually,"* accompanied by the sniggers of those around you.

If the word makes you feel uncomfortable, call it a *purpose*; we're happy with that and it is less likely to raise the cynic's eyebrows.

The *vision* or *purpose* the New South Wales (NSW) Police Service set in the early 90s is revealing: *"By the end of the decade NSW will have the safest streets in Australia"*.

This is a perfect example of the description "dream with a date". The NSW Police Service adeptly combined the *dream* of community safety, with a pragmatic time frame. No-one is left in doubt about the intent and no-one should have any doubts of the capacity of such an experienced group of law enforcement practitioners, given they understand their market, to devise a range of practical objectives and strategies to achieve it.

The *vision or purpose* for IKEA, probably Sweden's most famous export next to Volvo, may not fit the 'dream with a date' formula quite as well but it still reveals the way forward, and provides the organisation with absolute clarity of purpose: *"...to create a better everyday life for the many people"*.

The slightly incorrect grammatical structure makes it intriguing, perhaps reminding us of the company's Swedish heritage, and the fact that there is no time frame does not change the clarity of IKEA's intent: it applies today, tomorrow and well into the future. One of the long-term objectives of IKEA is to have a positive impact on people and the environment, and it has committed to minimising, or ideally, completely refraining from, the use of chemicals and substances in manufacture that can be harmful. IKEA holds itself accountable to the most rigorous health and safety testing of perhaps any organisation. It set an early ban on the use of PVC in everything except cables, and it banned all brominated organic flame retardants in furniture and formaldehyde emitting paints and lacquers on all products — a very impressive outcome indeed from a simple vision.

We don't know if people have the same problem with the word *mission* but its function is just as simple. The *mission* defines the "business" the organisation is in, the products or services offered and the customer needs that must be satisfied. Some mission statements do this very well; others fall a little short. You be the judge.

Today the NSW Police Service has a slightly different *purpose* or vision statement, but we suspect its mission is much the same today as it was in the previous decade.

Its revised vision or *purpose* is "*a safe and secure New South Wales*".

Its *mission* is "*strengthening the capability of the New South Wales Police Force to provide a safe and secure NSW through quality training, education and development*".

Its vision is clear and the proposed method to achieve it, by strengthening capacity through training and education, is equally clear.

IKEA has become a phenomenal success story in more than 30 countries around the world. The cynics will claim that it had a good product idea and capitalised on a marketplace that was looking for goods at a price. The cynics would be right, but they will have conveniently ignored the incredible amount of energy the key executives would have invested in planning, including defining a succinct mission that they then had to live up to.

This is the mission that IKEA shares with every employee and every customer: *"We shall offer a wide range of home furnishing items of good design and function, at prices so low the majority of people can afford to buy them"*.

The vision and mission of Avis show how it has shaped the business that Avis is today and how the two parts of the Avis story have been combined for real power:

The Avis vision

We will lead our industry by defining service excellence and building unmatched customer loyalty.

The Avis Mission

We will ensure a stress-free car rental experience by providing superior services that cater to our customers' individual needs ... always conveying the 'We Try Harder®' spirit with knowledge, caring and a passion for excellence.

In the end, of course, Avis couldn't escape the single most important value of its organisation: *We Try Harder*. There is no mention of the used car business in either the vision or the mission — and there doesn't need to be. Creating a *vision* and a *mission* and *defining the business* are separate steps in the strategic planning process that need to be carefully understood. Once you have considered them for your own business you will begin to clearly see how you will achieve your mission.

And that brings us squarely back to where we started with this part of the journey: What are the brand's values that will help us to deliver on the promise outlined in the mission?

20

Adding value to the dream

The kind of analysis or review undertaken by Townsend goes to the very heart of strategic planning and is crucial to understanding where the organisation is now, and where the organisation wants to be in the future. As part of the Avis corporate statement for internal and public consumption, the company publishes a list of the values that must be in place to achieve its goals. The mission of the company sets up the platform, but it is adherence to the values that will, ultimately, ensure that the organisation does not end up promising what it can't deliver. Bill Bernbach put it succinctly: *"It is always a mistake to make good advertising for a bad product"*. Read *'promises'* in place of the words *'good advertising'* and you will get our point.

The Avis mission is unequivocal:

We will ensure a stress-free car rental experience by providing superior services that cater to our customers' individual needs ... always conveying the 'We Try Harder®' spirit with knowledge, caring and a passion for excellence.

But, how will Avis ensure the experience is stress-free, and what are the superior services that will cater to its customers' needs?

Clearly, there needs to be a set of strategies, processes and protocols in place to make such a mission work. For starters, the product or service at the very heart of the brand must meet a set of criteria determined as the minimum requirement in consultation with customers. Because of the business Avis is in, its mission should begin with a standard of vehicles that is second to none. But product is only one part of the equation.

No matter what business you are in, there will be a 'people' component. Even if you don't consider yourself to be in the service business, take a closer look and you will find, through a tool such as the brandcycle, a point at which your employees can let you down, and let you down with potentially serious results.

If you haven't already done so, apply the brandcycle to your business. Consider each point of contact your customer has with your product or service and organisation. Ask yourself the tough question: *What can go wrong at that point?* Examine the personal relationship with your customer and what systems or processes are in place that could go wrong. And at each point ask yourself what steps you could take to make sure the experience remains first class.

Then examine the processes and the training systems you have in place, because unless they are capable of removing the potential risk, or creating the skills needed to maintain and sustain the product through its journey with your customer, you just may be wasting your time.

The processes that provide essential support to your business must be capable of consistent performance. Your product might be world-beating, but if your receptionist is having a bad day and is offhand or even rude to a customer, that interaction sours the goodwill already offered.

A bank officer going to extraordinary lengths to ensure a disaffected customer's loan application is treated with every care, in a spirit of true customer service, is let down if the papers prepared at head office arrive with the customer's name spelt incorrectly. Not only does it reinforce the customer's cynicism towards the bank, but the time taken to correct the mistake could make the customer late for another appointment. As a consequence the customer could get angry or frustrated at the officer who has tried so hard, and may voice this anger and frustration about the bank's poor customer ethos out loud, and to anyone who will listen.

So, even before you sit down to plan the strategy to deliver the promise, you need to establish the values that will make this possible.

Your brand values!

Once you have established a clear picture of who (or what) you are, and have created a vision and a mission that clearly articulates the direction you plan to take, you will need to examine that mission and how you plan to deliver it.

Each word in the Avis mission has been carefully considered, so that, even from the outside looking in, you can make a reasonable judgement on the brand values the company holds dear. That it is customer focused is without question, even without the reference to the *"We Try Harder spirit"*.

Avis makes no bones about its values: they are published on the internet, printed inside countless corporate brochures and manifestos and they probably hang in the sales offices, or sit framed on the service desk where you fill out the paperwork. If you haven't noticed them it's possibly because you have not had time to. If Avis is delivering on the promise of a stress-free car rental experience, you will have been in and out of the office quickly, efficiently, without waiting and certainly without time to be bothered reading company propaganda. (However, we must reassure you that this is not an advertisement for Avis; we are using the example as a case study, not affirming that every experience is stress-free.)

The values of Avis are wide-ranging, yet relevant. Nothing seems superfluous or patronising. Avis deals with integrity at the very start with a pledge to honour all commitments to customers, employees and shareholders. The company looks internally to its employees and acknowledges the need to deal with all equally and with respect, in the belief that these ideals will flow onto its customers. Avis reinforces its customer-centric focus with a commitment to quality and a restatement of its *We Try Harder* philosophy.

Teamwork is given noble status. Through team values Avis presents not only a unified approach for its customers, but offers employees growth and career opportunities and, in so doing, gives legitimacy to its right to pursue growth and profitability on behalf of shareholders. Finally, Avis acknowledges the critical importance of the community and the company's responsibilities as a good corporate citizen.

The cynic would argue that words and phrases such as *high standards of honesty, trust* and *open communication* are easy to say, but not so easy to implement.

And you know what? The cynics are right — if the company portrays such lofty ambitions and then FAILS to deliver, it is guilty of the worst, the most heinous crime any company can commit. It may seem inappropriate to some to put an advertising man up on a pedestal, but Bernbach was absolutely right, and the old maxim, *only promise something if you can deliver*, is sometimes the hardest lesson of all to learn.

> **Avis Values**
>
> **Integrity**
>
> - We will honour all commitments to our customers, employees and shareholders.
> - We will conduct business with unwavering high standards of honesty, trust, professionalism and ethical behaviour.
> - We will communicate openly and frequently, sharing what we know, when we know it.
>
> **Respect for the Individual**
>
> - We will treat each person with whom we work with respect, professionalism and dignity.
> - We will communicate expectations to employees, and provide honest and timely feedback on performance.
> - We will embrace a diversity of ideas, cultures, ethnicities, and backgrounds to enhance our promise and value to customers.
> - We will provide career development opportunities for employees who show initiative, and performance results to help them individually manage their careers to maximize their potential.
>
> **Quality**
>
> - We will place the interests of our customers first.
> - We will be dedicated to providing an individualized rental experience that assures customer satisfaction and earns the unwavering loyalty of our customers.

- We will ensure that the "We Try Harder®" philosophy underlies everything we do and shines through in our service to customers.

Teamwork

- We will work as one cohesive team from the smallest unit to the organization as a whole.
- We will develop and retain leaders who continually raise the bar, provide direction, remove barriers and empower people to successfully accomplish goals.
- We will maintain a caring and supportive work environment that fosters a sharing of ideas, skills and resources.

Growth and Profitability

- We will be dedicated to continuous innovation and pursue new ideas and opportunities to accelerate profitable growth.
- We will deliver value in all we do to assure consistently high returns to our shareholders.
- We will recognize and reward excellent performance, which drives superior results.

Community Responsibility

- We will be active participants in our communities and encourage employee involvement in civic and charitable activities.
- We will be role model business leaders in the countries and communities in which we operate.
- We will develop and implement business practices consistent with safeguarding the environment.

21
Committing to the dream

Remember why we came on this journey in the first place? From the opening lines of *Brand-aid* we have pursued the idea that every decision we make is made as a customer or consumer. In Chapter Two we articulated a clear definition of what a brand is and what it means to consumers. We contended that to consumers a "branded" product or service is greater than the sum of its tangible assets, and that we couldn't always define the intangible component as accurately as we would wish because it is so individual and personal to each consumer.

It was with this recognition that the true power of brands began to emerge, because brands build relationships. We said it at the start of the book, and it is timely to remind ourselves, that the brand is the very essence of the relationship built between consumers and the product or service, and those relationships are the very cornerstone of success for any company because they represent repeat business.

To have a strong brand, you must have the capacity to manage the image of the product or service so that it creates a desirable identity, greater than the sum of its parts. The aim must be to create a brand that, first and foremost, meets the consumer's 'What's in it for me?' expectation, secondly, that the consumer can relate to, and most importantly, that the consumer wants to build a 'repeat purchase relationship' with.

And the person who runs the company, be it the owner, founder, manager or CEO, must be ultimately responsible for the brand. This is the person who has to stand in front of the bank manager and plead for the extra overdraft to meet growth, and the person who has to stand in front of the board of directors and explain why the targets weren't met.

Richard Branson and Gail Kelly come from two distinctly different backgrounds and operate in two distinctly different arenas. One is head of an internationally respected airline; the other is head of a major bank operating in the Pacific Rim. Branson's first foray with the Virgin brand was a mail order business selling records, which culminated in a recording label, but his start was selling heavily discounted records from the boot of his car to retailers in the English high streets. Gail Kelly began her working career as a teacher in Rhodesia (Zimbabwe) before joining South Africa's Nedcor bank as a teller.

Ironically there are incredible similarities between the two.

Branson is one of the world's greatest entrepreneurs and one of its wealthiest people. He wasn't a strong academic performer at school, but excelled at sports. Under the Virgin brand he has achieved success in the record business, the airline business, the mobile phone business, the rail business and even the soft drink business. He is also possibly the first private entrepreneur in the space business, with Virgin Galactic.

In 2008, business journal *Forbes* rated Kelly the 11th most powerful woman in the world, a higher ranking than Hillary

Clinton, Oprah Winfrey and the British Queen. From her humble beginnings as a teller, Kelly's banking career took off when she was appointed as head of human resources at the Nedcor bank. This stellar performance was surpassed when she was put in charge of strategic marketing at Australia's Commonwealth Bank, one of this country's top four banks, and then she was promoted to run its Customer Service Division. Her skills and experience saw her land at St George Bank as CEO, before being offered the position of CEO at Westpac. Gail Kelly holds an arts degree with majors in Latin and history, as well as a diploma of education.

Where are the so-called similarities, we hear you mutter?

What Branson discovered as a young man was his capacity to connect with people. To his staff, he appears to be three things: a larger than life figure, a mentor, and just one of the "boys". From all reports his staff idolise him and he responds with respect and total support for the jobs they do. Outside the company he is constantly talking, discovering and evaluating. His primary source of opportunity comes from his awareness of other people's needs and his own intuitive sense of how to resolve those needs. In other words, Branson is the epitome of a brand leader.

Gail Kelly has spent almost her entire working life talking to people, and we assume, listening to them as well. Her training as a teacher ensures her commitment to sharing knowledge. The roles she has undertaken within the banking system have focused on the market need. Her performance as head of the branch network would have relied on her capacity to listen to customers, and her equally intuitive ability to resolve customer's needs.

Richard Branson has had more than his share of challenges. Virgin Rail has struggled to remain viable; his Virgin Vodka didn't quite meet the tastes of vodka drinkers; and he has had a number of other highly publicised failures. Yet he has managed to continue climbing and the pinnacle may well be in space.

Gail Kelly has enjoyed an illustrious career building some of the most public brands in Australia but is currently facing her greatest challenge as a result of a number of blunders having a heavy impact on the Westpac brand. When the interest rates cycle turned upwards at the end of the global financial crisis of 2008–2009, Westpac alone moved its rates above those set by Australia's Reserve Bank, and was excoriated by its customers, competitors and the government. It got worse when Westpac released an explanation of its position, saying, "We are not the Jetstar (discount airline) of the banking sector", and followed this up with an email animation comparing the cost of funds with the cost of bananas. Some wondered just who the monkeys were. So, succeed or fail, Kelly understands one thing: as CEO of Westpac, whatever happens to the brand is her responsibility.

Branson knows only too well that he embodies the Virgin brand in all its incarnations. He also respects the role of every member of the Virgin team in continuing to deliver the brand promise. He listens and he learns at every step from the people around him and the people his brands serve. The name of his brand is living testimony to this principle. Incidentally, Branson did not come up with the name *Virgin*; one of his employees suggested the name as living proof that they were all *virgins* in business.

Along this journey we have recognised the similarities between our key proposition and those espoused by some of the best business thinkers this world has seen. We have acknowledged that many of these principles run in parallel with each other and that some of the ideas from 50 years ago are as relevant today as they were then. By learning the lessons of others, and combining that with our own philosophy of branding, we have endeavoured to establish the steps that you need to take to create your own powerful brand and build repeat business.

We have carefully considered the question of what business you are in to open up, rather than restrict, your thinking on the brand. We have demonstrated how most organisations look at their product or service from the perspective of features and attributes, rather than the way consumers do, as benefits, or what's in it for them. And we have looked at the correlation between the way you present that brand and the values that must be consistently delivered to make sure the relationship stays strong.

So how do you implement those brand values throughout your organisation? How can you ensure that every contact a customer has with your brand is a positive experience that will build the relationship and encourage repeat purchase.

Consider the essence of your brand. Is it that dissimilar from the core part of your vision?

Nokia, the massive Finnish brand that dominates the world of mobile phones, has a very succinct vision: *"Our promise is to help people feel close to what is important to them"*. The strategy outlined on the company's website tells us that Nokia is a consumer-led company in a world experiencing ongoing increases in consumer involvement with technology and communications. The company's vision must be a direct response to the people who are broadening their modes of communication and want to be truly connected.

Nokia's strategy has been distilled into a brand essence of *connecting people*.

The brand essence of the tree, we concluded earlier, was a *supporter of life*; and in this time of enormous concern and worldwide speculation about climate change, there could not be a nobler calling, or a more emotional connection. A vision requires consideration of why we exist and where we want to be: the dream with a date. If we were writing the vision for a tree, could it be any more profound than: *Over the decades to come we promise to be a true supporter of life?* Could there be a better mission than: *We will provide the world with a natural and safe solution to the dangers of climate change through our capacity to convert CO_2 into life-giving oxygen?*

In small organisations it is a relatively straightforward exercise to commit to a vision and a mission. One or two people who share the same beliefs and similar attitudes can work in harmony to their end goal. The problem begins to emerge when the numbers involved start to increase.

Our experience in growing small businesses into medium-sized businesses underlines this dilemma. Every company going through different growth phases knows that a point will be reached at which it will be presented with a range of issues and problems that it will need to manage very carefully if the company is to continue growing. Management may be confronted with financial restrictions that the bank has put in the way of the next stage of expansion. Or the problem may simply be a housing issue, having outgrown the existing accommodation but without medium- to long-term projections to justify moving. Perhaps the next phase requires specific skills that your staff don't have and which will require significant reconfiguration of the human resources in the organisation. These kinds of dilemmas confront every business at some point, but they shift and change with the circumstances. The dilemma of internal communication is a constant at all stages of growth and is the greatest enemy of achieving your vision that we can think of.

We start off small, with an idealistic view of ourselves and the world. Our vision is sacrosanct; we have laboured hard to devise the product and service that is going to meet our customer's needs better than any other. We have carefully articulated the business we are in and the values that we hold dear, not just to our *new brand* but to our life. It is as clear as the smile on your face, and it is printed, indelibly, on our brain.

But you also need other people to commit to the vision and help you to achieve it.

Martin Luther King had no such problem. He envisioned a world without racial bigotry, and committed himself to this vision. His commitment was so strong, and his belief so profound, that he shared that vision with hundreds of thousands, in fact, millions of people. Almost 50 years on, there are vast numbers of people who are still able to recite, some, or all, of Martin Luther King's vision.

Perhaps if he hadn't committed his vision to paper and allowed the media to transmit his text around the world, he wouldn't have had to pay the ultimate penalty, his life.

And immediately, we imagine the cynics rise to the surface and start throwing barbs at us, rebuking us for even daring to quote the vision of a man as great as Martin Luther King.

If you agree with the cynics, then consider this: Did Richard Branson become one of the wealthiest and most influential men in the world without a vision of what he could achieve, and without the framework necessary to build a great and enduring brand? Can you separate Richard Branson, the man, from Virgin? Of course you can't.

Can you separate Bill Gates from Microsoft, and are you going to tell us that Bill Gates didn't have a powerful vision behind the creation of his brand, which is now used in 80 per cent of computers around the world? Separate Mao Zedong from China, or Ghandi from India? You can't.

Of course, the cynics may return and laugh at the small business owner, struggling to pay an overdraft, juggling HR decisions with marketing strategies and they ask: Are you serious, do you truly believe that you can achieve the same as a Richard Branson?

Our answer is a swift and unrelenting, YES!

How else could Richard Branson have done what he has done unless he started somewhere? From what we know, Bill Gates wasn't born with a silver spoon in his mouth, but with a vision in his heart.

So what did they do better than the people who didn't reach the same lofty heights? They articulated the business they believed they were in; they articulated the values that would help them achieve their goals; and from those attributes they constructed a powerful brand capable of carrying that message to the world. And then they communicated at every step of their journey; they committed themselves to a vision that never wavered; and they made sure that everyone who worked with them on their journey understood every aspect of that vision.

Earlier, in Chapter 18, we reviewed a colleague's balloon printing business with the aid of what we have called the 5 p's of brand value. Our colleague is like so many small or medium enterprises, confronted with the dilemmas of growth and expansion. In fact, he may be in more trouble than he thinks, and is probably, right now, trying to answer the one question that will get him focused on his vision.

While our colleague's company name, Better Balloons, defines his core business, to date we are not so sure that this is the business he is in, moving forward. Whereas balloons have defined him in the past, he sees his future in the broader area of printing, using the digital technologies he so effectively applies to balloons. That same technology enables him to print on to any surface: plastic, paper, rubber, metal, even ceramic. Onto those surfaces he prints advertising material to go with live events or at the point of sale.

How does he invest this broader scope into a name such as "Better Balloons"? With great difficulty, we would suggest. His brand name has a specificity about it that limits his capacity to expand the customer's understanding of what his business does. Compounding the problem is a decision being contemplated by our colleague to move his business to a busier location in order to achieve greater visibility among his prospects. But who, in the future, are his prospects? Are they the same group of people that he founded his business to serve? Do they have the same needs?

We would argue that unless our colleague makes the right decisions, based on a clearly articulated vision, he will struggle to emulate Branson or Gates and build a truly powerful brand. And unless he is able to articulate what his brand means and the values that stand behind it, he will always struggle to get his employees to share in his vision and help his business grow.

References

1. Interbrand. (2008). *Interbrand Best Global Brands 2008*. Retrieved 30 November 2009 from http://www.interbrand.com/best_global_brands.aspx 2009 rankings are up on this website now]
2. Anon, (2009, November 18). Australia's Most Valuable Brands. *Business Review Weekly*
3. Keller, K.L. (1996). *Strategic Brand Management: Building and Managing Brand Equity*. Prentice Hall: Englewood Cliffs, NJ.
4. Kapferer, J.N. (1992). *Strategic Brand Management*. Free Press: New York.
5. Upshaw, L. (1995). *Building Brand Identity*. John Wiley & Sons: New York.
6. Paul Budde Communications. (2008). *2008 Global Mobile Communications – Statistics, trends and forecasts*. Retrieved 30 November 2009 from http://www.marketresearch.com/product/display.asp?productid=1687234
7. Carswell, A. (2009, October 27). Westpac group executive Peter Hanlon admits shutting down bank branches was wrong. *The Daily Telegraph*.
8. Millward Brown. (2009). *Brandz Top 100 Most Valuable Global Brands 2009*. Retrieved 30 November 2009 from http://

www.millwardbrown.com/Sites/Optimor/Content/KnowledgeCenter/BrandzRanking.aspx

9   This data, along with Millward Brown's complex methodology for establishing global brand value can be accessed at http://www.millwardbrown.com

10 Roll, M. (2006). *Asian Brand Strategy*. Palgrave MacMillan: New York.

11 *"While we may justifiably take pride in having built the largest food product business in the country, we do not pause to rest upon our laurels. In all that we do, and will do, we never forget that we face an increasingly competitive environment. In this environment, we have survived and grown on the basis of our greatest strength: co-operative culture, co-operative networking, market acumen and respect for both producer and the consumer."* AMUL vision statement. Retrieved 30 November 2009 from http://www.amul.com/index1.html

12 p. 79 in Bellur, V.V., Singh, S.P., Chaganti, Radharao, & Chaganti, Rajeswararao. (1990). The White Revolution: How AMUL brought milk to India. *Long Range Planning*, 23(6):71-79.

13 Dowling, J. (2003, September 19). Volvo battle gets bloody. *Drive*. Retrieved 30 November 2009 from http://www.drive.com.au/Editorial/ArticleDetail.aspx?ArticleID=4571&vf=1

14 Kotler, P. et al. (1994). *Marketing.* [is this *Marketing: Australia and New Zealand*?]Prentice Hall: Frenchs Forrest, NSW.

15 Nagourney, A. (2008, November 3). The '08 Campaign: Sea Change for Politics as We Know It. *The New York Times*. This case study is drawn from: McCarthy, R. (2009). How Barack Obama networked a nation. In J. Harrison (2009) (ed.), *Case studies of communication campaigns using Web 2.0:*

From the biggest job in the world to the best job in the world, 25-45.

16 Teinowitz, I. (2008, July 23). Olympic Deal Sealed: Obama Makes $5 Million Buy, *Advertising Age*.

17 MSNBC. (2008, October 9). *Obama plans prime-time TV ad before Nov. 4*. Retrieved April 10, 2009, from http://www.msnbc.msn.com/id/27107689/

18 p. 562 in Williams, A.P., & Trammell, K.D., (2005). Candidate Campaign E-Mail Messages in the Presidential Election 2004. *American Behavioral Scientist*, 49(4):560-574.

19 Chan, D. (2000). The story of Singapore Airlines and the Singapore Girl. *Journal of Management Development*, 19(6):456-472, and Chan, D. (2000). Beyond Singapore Girl: Grand and product/service differentiation strategies in the new millennium. *Journal of Management Development*, 19(6):515-542.

20 As above, p. 459.

21 As above, p. 460.

22 Levitt, T. (1960). Marketing Myopia. *Harvard Business Review*, 38(4):45-56.

23 De Bono, E. (2000). *Six Thinking Hats.* Penguin: Harmondsworth, UK.

24 Roy Morgan Research. (2009, May 18). *Roy Morgan Research tracking poll looks at small business customer satisfaction with banks since 2003*. Retrieved 30 November 2009 from http://www.roymorgan.com/news/press-releases/2009/883.

25 Maslow, A. (1943). A Theory of Human Motivation. *Psychological Review*, 50(4):370-396.

26 Evans, M. (2009, December 10). How the top banana slipped. *Sydney Morning Herald*.

27 Carlzon, J. (1989). *Moments of Truth*. Harper Collins: New York.

28 Rich, S. (2009, October 19). CEOs learn the customer is frighteningly right. *The Australian*.

29 As above.

30 MacMillan, I.C., & McGrath, R.G. (1997). Discovering New Points of Differentiation. *Harvard Business Review*, 75(4):133-45.

31 Benns, M. (2009). *The men who killed Qantas*. William Heinemann: Melbourne.